City, Save Thyself!

Nuclear Terror and the Urban Ballot

In *City, Save Thyself!*, David A. Wylie proposes introducing a new voice into the process of saving the world from nuclear destruction — cities. In multinational conferences and proto-parliaments, he sees cities exerting their influence to shape national policies. In so doing, he contrasts what he feels is the democratic base of cities with the corporate base of federal governments. To be sure, there are such cities, though by no means not all, and the process Wylie outlines could exercise a beneficial influence on national policies, as can transnational non-governmental organizations and Web alliances. In the task of moving the nations of the world away from nuclear weapons, cities might be a new source of power which commentators up to now have ignored.

—**Craig Eisendrath,** *former State Department official, co-founder of the National Constitution Center, and presently chairman of the Project for Nuclear Awareness*

I have read with great interest the book "*City, Save Thyself!*." I fully agree that global peace must be rooted in the local communities.

—**Hans Köchler,** *Univ.-Prof. Dr. Dr. h.c., Institut für Philosophie der Universität Innsbruck*

The analysis of David Wylie in *City, Save Thyself! Nuclear Terror and the Urban Ballot* creatively illuminates one example of the growing significance of local governments in the development of global governance. It is responsive to the fact that people everywhere are ever more linked around the world in their daily lives. After assessing the threat of smuggled nuclear devices, Wylie provides a detailed strategy on how local governments can cope with this problem. The volume concludes with very helpful examples of letters, resolutions and agendas that will be useful to local citizens who would like to become involved.

—**Chadwick F. Alger,** *Mershon Professor of Political Science and Public Policy Emeritus, Ohio State University.*

City, Save Thyself! faces squarely the changed historical situation that the threat of nuclear war and nuclear terrorism present, rendering the towns and cities where most of us live not ultimately defensible. It sees the global leadership that we have undertaken since 1945 beginning to strain our democracy. Then it constructs a politically passionate argument for updating the Madison, Hamilton, Jay Federalist explication of American constitutionalism. Its ideas for tapping the real and decent democracy of our municipal life and giving it a role in our foreign and international relations are novel and practical. They have a real bearing on what Lincoln understood as the "last best hope of earth."

—**Prof. Joseph Preston Baratta,** *Ph.D., Associate Professor, Worcester State College*

City, Save Thyself!

Nuclear Terror and the Urban Ballot

DAVID A. WYLIE

Trueblood
Publishing

Published by Trueblood Publishing Co. LLC
One State Street, Suite 1500,
Boston, MA 02109

Distributed to the book trade by Small Press United, a division of
Independent Publishers Group
814 North Franklin Street, Chicago, IL 60610
To order, call 1 800 888 4741 or email to orders@ipgbook.com

ISBN 978-1-935506-07-2 (softbound)
ISBN 978-1-935506-08-9 (hardbound)

Library of Congress Control Number: 2009935844

Designed, produced, and edited by Vern Associates, Inc. www.vernassoc.com

The text paper is Rolland Enviro100, an acid-free, 100 percent recycled
PCW sheet.

Printed in the United States of America

Photo credits:
Front cover inset photos, clockwise from lower left:
Larry Mayer/Creatas/Jupiterimages
Perry Mastrovito/Creatas/Jupiterimages
Polka Dot Images/Jupiterimages
Digital Vision/Jupiterimages

Front cover: Earth Observatory, NASA

CONTENTS

DEDICATION

To my granddaughters Grace Wylie and Chloe Wylie

ACKNOWLEDGMENTS

The thoughts in this volume owe everything to the hundreds of political workers who helped me through thirteen political campaigns, and my colleagues in Cambridge municipal government, who helped me explore how cities and towns might be harnessed for the world's forbidding future. More exploratory thinking was facilitated by my years on the boards of Coalition for a Strong U.N., and Lawyers Alliance for World Security. The Boston Athenaeum and its staff were always helpful in research.

Peter Blaiwas and Brian Hotchkiss of Vern Associates for their first-rate editorial, design, and production assistance. Suzanne Manness, Suzanne Pearce, and Joan Powell provided expert editing assistance. Steve Carlson served as a consultant, David Whitty and Bill Allen read chapters and furnished advice. Jim Anker gave business advice. Ken Martin provided a photo. At Newman Communications, David Overton served as publicist. The Small Press United division of Independent Publishers Group, Mark Suchomel, President, undertook distribution.

My assistant for 35 years, Melissa Sachs is always there. My wife Kathy Neilson made commitment tolerable.

I also am grateful to Bill Latimer, former editor of *The Bolton Common*, and the *Common's* former publishers Kathleen Cushman and Edward Miller, who let me explore over three years some of the thoughts that became central to this book, in a weekly column that I called, "Basic Assumptions." It upset some of their readers to have it suggested that views on zoning, town budgets, and public education, and views on weapons and war, rest on the same basic assumptions about human nature and the capacity of law to order society. To some, it proved unsettling as well to read that if we each would be aware of our basic assumptions, own up to them, and exercise allegiance to them through the ballot box rather than shouting down, or shooting down, the opposition, there might yet be hope.

PART I

WHY NOW?

Since the first atomic bomb was detonated in Alamogordo, New Mexico, in 1945, many have feared that terrorists might obtain a nuclear weapon and destroy nations. The expectation remained theoretical so long as the U.S.–U.S.S.R. dual checkmate kept the technology secure. Over the twenty years since the Soviet Union's breakup, however, we have seen theft from the Russian stockpile, a nuclear black market, A. Q. Khan's boost to proliferation, America's neglect of its obligations under the Non-Proliferation Treaty, the Middle East cauldron, and 9/11. Today, almost sixty-five years after Alamogordo, many U.S. government officials think nuclear capability among terrorist groups is imminent. Most Americans have paid little heed because the Iraq invasion, which was predicated on the false claim that Iraq had weapons of mass destruction, discredited the government. Euphoria over Barack Obama's 2008 election victory threatens to prolong citizen unconcern due to unwarranted confidence that somehow more responsible U.S. governance will cause this and other nations to do what nations have never done—adopt effective arms control. Part I of this book assesses whether we should be worried enough about nuclear proliferation and terrorism to undertake novel action.

But of all al-Qa'ida's efforts to obtain other forms of WMD, the main threat is the nuclear one. I am convinced that this is where UBL [Usama bin Laden] and his operatives desperately want to go. They understand that bombings by cars, trucks, trains, and planes will get them some headlines, to be sure. But if they manage to set off a mushroom cloud, they will make history. Such an event would place al-Qa'ida on a par with the superpowers and make good bin Laden's threat to destroy our economy and bring death into every American household. . . . The terrorists are endlessly patient. The first plans to attack the World Trade Center were made a decade before the Twin Towers fell. . . . One mushroom cloud would change history. My deepest fear is that this is exactly what they intend. (Tenet 2007, 279–80)

—George Tenet, director of the Central Intelligence Agency under presidents Bill Clinton and George W. Bush

CHAPTER 1

Throw out the Lifeline

Under many houses, people screamed for help. . . .
The wounded limped past the screams. . . . (Hersey
1946, 40)

[H]e brought two horribly wounded people—a
woman with a whole breast sheared off and a man
whose face was all raw from a burn—to share the
simple shed with her. No one came back. (Hersey
1946, 44)

He reached down and took a woman by the hands,
but her skin slipped off in huge, glove-like pieces.
(Hersey 1946, 60)

When he penetrated the bushes, he saw there were
about twenty men, and they were all in exactly the
same nightmarish state: their faces were wholly
burned, their eye sockets were hollow, and the fluid
from their melted eyes had run down their cheeks.
(Hersey 1946, 68)

> *She kept the small corpse in her arms for four days,*
> *even though it began smelling bad on the second*
> *day. (Hersey 1946, 76)*

> *[M]addened people were running like demented*
> *lemmings, trying to get across the river. They were*
> *screaming, and it sounded like one enormous voice.*
> *In the middle of the bridge lay four or five bodies,*
> *unrecognizable as human beings, but still moving.*
> *Their skin hung from them like strands of dark sea-*
> *weed! Instead of noses, holes! There were still fifty*
> *or sixty clinging to the red-hot rails. In their ter-*
> *ror of dying they clawed their way over one another,*
> *their eyes hanging from their sockets, pushing one*
> *another into the river, and screaming all the time.*
> *(Jungk 1961, 207)*

Will these accounts from Hiroshima, Japan, after the nuclear bombing of August 6, 1945, be replayed in Atlanta, Milwaukee, Dallas, San Francisco, Philadelphia, or all these and maybe more cities? If George Tenet, the one American who as CIA director under two presidents ought to know, says that the folks who outfoxed our superpower spy system and smashed two immense towers to the ground want to burn out my eyes, then I am worried. And Tenet is not the only terrified insider:

- State Department counterterrorism coordinator: More terror attacks are only a question of time.

- Los Alamos scientist: Terrorist use of nuclear or radiological weapons is going to happen.

- British Intelligence heads: Are positive Islamic terrorists will use a radiological bomb or other WMD on London or another Western city.

- Former chief negotiator for the Safe and Secure Disman-tlement of Nuclear Weapons: Defense against terrorists with nuclear weapons cannot succeed indefinitely as more nations acquire them.

- University specialist (subsequently appointed by President Obama to Under Secretary of Defense for Acquisition, Technology and Logistics): Hiroshima was only a glimpse of what will happen when terrorists are nuclear equipped.

- Academic: Nothing after that will resemble today's social order.

- Director of Emergency Response at the National Nuclear Security Administration: The only question is when the terrorist nuclear attack will come.

- Former Secretary of State: A nuclear Pearl Harbor will change the world "so dramatically that we will not recognize it."

- Director of the Defense Threat Reduction Agency: A nuclear weapon in a U.S. city is the worst nightmare keeping U.S. leaders awake at night.

- Discovery Institute fellow: We shall be scarred permanently by even one nuclear attack.

- Homeland Security undersecretary: A single terrorist nuclear yield will change history.

- Director of the University of Georgia Institute for Health Management and Mass Destruction Defense: The risk of a terrorist nuclear attack has grown over five years and increases yearly, as a ten-kiloton bomb can easily be smuggled in via land, sea, or air.

- Pakistani physicist: It is quite possible jihadists will seize Pakistan nuclear weapons or materials.

- Homeland Security undersecretary: Maritime shipping is vulnerable to sneaking WMD into a U.S. city.

- Former Australian foreign minister: "We are on the brink of. . . an avalanche or a cascade of proliferation. . . . Each new country that goes nuclear increases the danger of a terror group gaining a nuclear bomb. . . . I don't think the world really understands how serious the consequences are of a terrorist setting off a nuclear bomb in one of our cities. . . the 100,000 dead are just the beginning."

- Commission on the Prevention of WMD Proliferation and Terrorism: "Terrorists are determined to attack us again— with weapons of mass destruction if they can. . . . Our margin of safety is shrinking, not growing. . . . It is more likely than not that a weapon of mass destruction will be used in a terrorist attack somewhere in the world by the end of 2013."*

Naturally, I expect my superpower government to protect me. I look at its success over sixty-five years in building more and bigger bombs and rockets. Then I look at its failure to

* Attributions for bulleted items listed here are, sequentially: Henry Crumpton, *London Daily Telegraph*, Nuclear Threat Initiative's Global Security Newswire (NTI/GSN), January 17, 2006; Chris Morris, *San Francisco Chronicle* (NTI/GSN), May 8, 2006; British Intelligence, *Sunday Daily Telegraph* (NTI/GSN), June 26, 2006; James Goodby, *Baltimore Sun* (NTI/GSN), February 5, 2007; Ashton Carter of Harvard University, *San Francisco Chronicle* (NTI/GSN), May 11, 2007; Steve Fetter of University of Maryland, *San Francisco Chronicle* (NTI/GSN), May 11, 2007; Deborah Wilber, *Los Angeles Times* (NTI/GSN), January 7, 2008; George Shultz (NTI/GSN), February 26, 2008; James Tegnelia, Senate Armed Services Emerging Threats and Capabilities Subcommittee testimony (NTI/GSN), March, 13, 2008; John Wohlstetter, United Press International (NTI/GSN), March 26, 2008; Charles Allen, *Asian News International/ Daily India* (NTI/GSN), April 7, 2008; Cham Dallas, Senate Homeland Security and Governmental Affairs Committee testimony (NTI/GSN), April 16, 2008; Pervez Hoodbhoy, Indo-Asian News Service (NTI/GSN), May 12, 2008; Charles Allen (NTI/GSN), October 8, 2008; Gareth Evans, remarks to reporters at first meeting of International Commission on Nuclear Nonproliferation and Disarmament (NTI/GSN), October 21, 2008; *World at Risk: Report of the Commission on the Prevention of WMD Proliferation and Terrorism* (New York: Vintage Books, 2008), pp. xii, xiii, xv.

prevent emulation by other governments. Then I consider that terrorists are suicidal and mobile, not targetable and deterrable. And that al-Qaeda claims the right to kill four million Americans, including one million children, as payback for American depredations against Muslims (Tenet 2007, 269). All this makes me reflect that the terrorists are sustained by facts that I have no means to dispute. Terrorists say that I help maintain a government and economy and military policy that exploit other people. If I maintain a nation that invites others to visit upon me and my family the inhuman fate of burned-out eyes and shredded skin, it seems as though I should consider whether policies that incite hatred are really in the national interest.

I do not feel compelled to figure out what American policies should have been followed during sixty-five years of nuclear weapons buildup and proliferation, what was done right and what wrong, and what alternatives existed. I do feel compelled to ask what ought to be done now. As I am an American thought to hold an allocation of democratic power over immense destructive resources, I feel compelled to question whether that reputed power allocation is real, and if it is not, how to reclaim it and what to do with it.

Little as I understand the terrorist mind, I want to know what American policies might prove equivalent to its cunning, a cunning inspired by fanaticism. The 9/11 pilots figured out just which half of flying they had to learn—the takeoff half! Saving time by neglecting the landing half of learning to fly, they somehow correctly surmised that their bizarre lesson plan would never get reported, or believed, or acted upon.

I want to match wits with those pilots. They decided that the Muslim nations, notably Saudi Arabia, had sold out what they cared about. They sought power that would prove comparable to national power and to my citizen's democratic power. The blunt truth, though, is that my democratic power over national policy is close to zero, because big money, big media,

and the gerrymander have reduced the influence of my opinions, reduced my chances to convince others of my views, and
diluted my vote. How can I retrieve the power of discourse,
persuasion, and action that democracy is supposed to confer?
If presidential political campaigns tiptoe around the terrorist
issue, as the 2008 campaign certainly did, and polls show a public not greatly alarmed, what can be done?

To be sure, defensive steps are under way. Radiation scan-
ning equipment is being installed at border posts and ports
around the world. Thousands of personnel receive disaster
training in simulated attack exercises. But stories of nuclear
smuggling appear almost daily. Smugglers are tried and jailed.
Suspects are tortured.

The Nuclear Non-Proliferation Treaty is currently undermined by the nuclear-technology ambitions of Iran and North
Korea, by elevating trade with India to a higher priority than
insisting that it adhere to the nonproliferation regime and by the
unwillingness of the United States and other current possessors to give up their nuclear weapons. That treaty, in effect since
1970, binds 188 nations to negotiate in good faith to achieve a
nuclear weapons "treaty on general and complete disarmament
under strict and effective international control" (Article VI).

More and more nations are building nuclear energy reactors, usually with no requirement that weapons-grade plutonium
be separated from spent fuel. By 2020, the present thirty-one
nuclear-power-producing nations will be joined by eighteen
more. Portable tactical nuclear weapons scattered around Russia "that terrorists would pay millions to get their hands on" are
exempt from the Nunn-Lugar program to secure the Cold War
arsenal of the former Soviet Union (Goodby 2007).

This book suggests that where political power, potentially
of national dimension, does remain accessible to American citizens is in the towns and cities in which we live. We need to use
it internationally, in cooperation with other towns and cities
around the world.

CHAPTER 2

Sixty-Five Years and Counting

Terrorist nuclear plots, though inconceivable to most before 9/11, have long been foretold. In *Must We Hide?*, published in 1949, R. E. Lapp eerily placed his example of what might happen a few blocks from 9/11's Ground Zero:

> Let us now turn our attention to a bomb smuggled into a city and detonated in the basement of a skyscraper. Certainly no newspaper reader has missed hearing the term suitcase warfare. . . . Assume that an atomic bomb is detonated in the basement of the City Hall at the lower end of Manhattan. (Lapp 1949, 80)

> The lesson is more than clear. It is not necessary to cite further details about Manhattan. Such cities are cities of the past. In an Atomic Age no nation can afford to present such a perfect target to an enemy. This will not be good news to property owners on the fabulous island but perhaps it is better to have property values change gradually over a period of years than to have the change come abruptly when the first bomb drops. (Lapp 1949, 85)

David R. Barash and Judith Eve Lipton described the effect of small-scale thefts of bomb components, many dozens of which have been reported since their *Stop Nuclear War! A Handbook* was published in 1982:

> Would-be nuclear terrorists would not have to recreate the Manhattan Project in order to get a bomb or two; there is no more secret. . . . One option for a would-be nuclear terrorist, then, is to accumulate plutonium or highly enriched uranium over a period of time, so that the losses are hidden in the statistic "noise" of accidental MUF [missing unaccounted for]. . . . Enough plutonium to blow up a large city could easily be smuggled anywhere by one person in the pockets of his coat. A one kiloton, do-it-yourselfer's delight, exploded just outside the restricted-access area during the State of the Union address, could kill everyone in the Capitol building. . . and bombs can easily be made small enough to fit inside a large suitcase, or placed in the trunk of a car parked innocuously at a curb. (Barash and Lipton 1982, 254–56)

In *Plutonium, Power, and Politics*, Gene I. Rochlin reported thirty years ago that "[t]here are nonstate adversaries in the world today who probably are capable of stealing fissionable material, or arranging for its theft" (Rochlin 1979, 355).

Twenty-five years ago Walter Patterson said in *The Plutonium Business and the Spread of the Bomb* that the potential nuclear thieves and bomb-makers included not only unscrupulous governments but also criminals, terrorists, and lunatics, many judged capable of obtaining bomb material, fabricating a bomb, and detonating it (Patterson 1984, 75).

James Adams, in *Engines of War*, observed, "Conflict can generally be viewed as an escalatory process where terrorists operate at the lowest end, rising through guerrilla warfare, conventional wars and finally to a war involving nuclear weapons" (Adams 1990, 272).

The U.S.S.R. tested its first atomic bomb in August 1949. The Korean War began in June 1950. Just prior to these and other events that produced the Cold War, strong bipartisan congressional support existed for international peacekeeping. Hearings were held though no vote was ever taken on House Concurrent Resolution 64 and identical Senate Concurrent Resolution 56, which stated that it should be a "fundamental objective" of U.S. foreign policy to develop the United Nations into a "world federation, open to all nations, with defined and limited powers adequate to preserve peace and prevent aggression through the enactment, interpretation, and enforcement of world law" (Baratta 2004, 578). The 111 House cosponsors included such noteworthy Republicans as Jacob Javits (New York), Christian A. Herter (Massachusetts), Gerald R. Ford (Michigan), and Walter H. Judd (Minnesota) as well as Democrats including John F. Kennedy (Massachusetts), Henry M. Jackson (Washington), Abraham Ribicoff (Connecticut), and Mike Mansfield (Montana). The 21 Senate cosponsors included Republicans Henry Cabot Lodge, Jr. (Massachusetts), Charles W. Tobey (New Hampshire) and Wayne Morse (Oregon) and Democrats Hubert Humphrey (Minnesota), John Sparkman and Lister Hill (Alabama), and B. Russell Long (Louisiana).

The Cold War made it politically unsupportable to search for solutions to nuclear war's no-winners curse, and the end of the Cold War brought little change to the content of international discourse on nuclear proliferation. Today the instincts and the language for international law enforcement that seemed a natural progression to past American leaders of all persuasions—and not in the least inconsistent with patriotism, freedom, and security—remain squelched. Three hundred million strong, free, rich, and "super" strong, we find ourselves with no response to the terrorist nuclear threat other than ringing the globe with seven hundred to a thousand military bases, according to

Chalmers Johnson in *Nemesis: The Last Days of the American Republic*. Johnson quotes a white paper from the neoconservative American Enterprise Institute that argues that the bases make of the U.S. military a

> global cavalry of the twenty-first century. . . . Among the many
> components in this transformation is the radical overhaul of
> America's overseas force structure, which seeks to create a
> worldwide network of frontier forts. . . [for the] preemption of
> terrorism. . . . Like the cavalry of the old west. . . [t]he realign-
> ment of our network of overseas bases into a system of fron-
> tier stockades is necessary to win a long-term struggle against
> an amorphous enemy across the arc of instability. (Johnson
> 2006, 148)

One wonders whether West Point cadets are taught frontiersmanship. Certainly the United States has placed its security reliance almost exclusively on weapons systems, deterrence, and power balancing. The public became persuaded that success at military dominance displaced the need to sacrifice anything of the political, economic, social, and even personal agendas on which our habits and success depend.

To reinforce this hallucination, leaders steeped themselves and most Americans in a patriotic mythology that conflated nuclear with moral attainments and concluded that each justified the other with deterrence our exclusive strategy. No head of state, cabinet member, administrator, or legislator has staked a career on plans to end the stupendous risks of nuclear arming.

The pursuit of military dominance has eclipsed public awareness that the world is too large and complex for one nation or group of nations to dominate and that policies aimed at dominance infuriate so many in other lands that security weakens. In fact, the flimsy justification of security through armaments masked, at best, economic stimulation, and, at worst, profiteering. The diligence with which the financial and political rewards of weapons production were proliferated through all fifty states speaks for itself.

Under President Reagan, the United States admittedly produced weapons based on a motivation that was secondary, at best, to security, but never secondary to profit-making. We sought to drive the Soviet Union into insolvency through an arms race centered on nuclear weapons, and, according to David Stockman, director of the Office of Management and Budget under Reagan, spent extravagantly on defense in order to squeeze social welfare spending out of the budget. If the worst comes, to have stimulated WMD production not only as a profit center, which would be bad enough, but also in pursuit of economic and political warfare, surely will prove the worst of all history's bad judgments.

Now, numerous leaders and observers in countries around the world assert that terrorist groups possess nuclear weapons, groups that cannot readily be targeted because of their dispersed locations and mobility. Deterrence, the fail-safe justification for sixty-five years of recklessness, is an anachronism.

War has destroyed civilizations, religions, politi-
cal institutions; but it has also won and preserved
them. And, as for myself, I thank the good God who
has given us bodies and souls strong and enduring
enough to win and hold them by war, so long as it
can be done in no other way. The whole question lies
in that. Has the time come, or is it near at hand,
when great international wars must of necessity
destroy more than they save? If so, then every such
war means a step backwards toward the extinction
of what we want to save.

—General Tasker Howard Bliss, Army chief of staff, 1917;
American representative on the Supreme War Council,
1917; member of the American Peace Commission, 1918.
(Palmer 1934, 445)

CHAPTER 3

Assessing the Threat

George W. Bush's spurious claim about weapons of mass destruction in Iraq was momentous beyond its falsity. Power holders were admitting what arms-control advocates have counseled since 1945: that a nuclear arms race would put strong countries at the mercy of small countries and terrorists. However, although this admission gave arms-control advocates a chance to press for comprehensive security measures, the opportunity was squandered. The prospect of WMD in the hands of a Saddam Hussein, let alone the events of 9/11, should have prompted rational discourse about vulnerability. It should have discredited conservative ideology about American singularity in military strength. But the government hurried to reconstruct the delusion that military strength ensures security, bolstered by the claim that American virtue should justify, in the eyes of the world, maintaining "super" strength.

"Rational discourse" about the ultimate inhumanity of nuclear terror verges on the contradictory. Perhaps that is why sixty-five years vanished with no serious effort to guarantee that nuclear horror would end with Hiroshima and Nagasaki. No leader risks telling people flat out that survival depends on radical change.

The Scope of Overexposure

In *The Al Qaeda Connection*, Paul L. Williams recalls that in the mid-1990s, with American assistance provided under the Nunn-Lugar Soviet Nuclear Threat Reduction Act of 1991, twenty-two thousand Soviet-era nuclear weapons were shifted to secure sites from forward deployment and locations in the fourteen newly independent republics. But at that time, as Williams comments, "everything in Russia was falling apart" (Williams 2005, 82). Unemployment hit 30 percent, inflation 2,000 percent, food shortages prevailed, life expectancy fell, the suicide rate jumped, and living conditions deteriorated, especially for military personnel. According to Williams, "In 1993 there were 6,430 reports of stolen weapons from army arsenals, ranging from assault rifles to tanks. It is incredible to assume that the twenty-two thousand nuclear weapons were moved from strategic sites to arsenals throughout Russia without a single loss" (Williams 2005, 83). U.S. Secretary of Defense Dick Cheney commented that if 90 percent of the 22,000 were recovered, that would represent "excellent performance" (Williams 2005, 83). Williams goes on to recount well-documented reports, few of which appeared in the press, that al-Qaeda bought small nuclear weapons through Chechen and other black market sources, including twenty "suitcase" nukes.

The amount of known smuggling of fissile material is variously reported. According to William Langewiesche in *The Atomic Bazaar*, "since the breakup of the Soviet Union, the International Atomic Energy Agency (IAEA) has reported seventeen officially declared cases of trafficking in plutonium or HEU, generally Russian-made" (Langewiesche 2007, 24). On September 26, 2008, the IAEA reported that 1,340 incidents of unauthorized use, possession, theft, and loss of nuclear materials had been reported from 1993 through 2007, including eighteen incidents of highly enriched uranium or plutonium (Wehle 2008).

Reporting some 250 nuclear or radioactive material thefts in the year ending in June 2008, director general of the IAEA

Mohamed ElBaradei said, "the possibility of terrorists obtaining nuclear or other radioactive material remains a grave threat" (*New York Times*, October 28, 2008).

Eleven million cargo containers enter the United States every year. The number scanned for radiation has steadily increased. Homeland Security claims that 98 percent of incoming cargo, all vehicles crossing southern borders, and 98 percent crossing from Canada receive radiation screening. (Global Security Newswire July 24, 2009).

In 58 foreign ports progress is being made in shifting from selective screening of U.S. bound cargoes, based on whether shipping manifests reflect high risk cargo, to the use, at five of the ports now, of drive-through portals that scan every container. (Global Security Newswire June 29 and July 24, 2009).

American strategy to counter the threat of smuggled nuclear devices was in disarray as the Obama administration took office. Congress had passed a law requiring that by 2012 all U.S.–bound maritime cargo be screened. Former Homeland Security Secretary Michael Chertoff declined to pursue the mandated goal (*Boston Globe*, November 8, 2008). President Obama's new Homeland Security Secretary Janet Napolitano, testified before the House Homeland Security Committee on February 24, 2009, the congressionally mandated deadline would not be achieved (*Boston Globe*, February 26, 2009).

Peter D. Zimmerman and Jeffrey G. Lewis (2006) say that the simplest al-Qaeda path is to acquire a 150-acre ranch in the U.S. West, adapt the barn and outbuildings into laboratories and mini-factories, and use a surplus artillery barrel, or recoilless rifle, as the basic building block. The first device would cost five to ten million dollars. The enriched uranium, imported in batches, would cost three to five million dollars. Payroll, for a physicist, a metallurgist, a machinist, an electronics engineer, and some assistants—perhaps nineteen people in all, no more than could be housed in the ranch house—would be one

million dollars. Add a vacuum furnace for $50,000, the gun bar-
rel for $10,000, the ranch for $150,000 with another $50,000 for
improvements, and so forth. The device, about nine feet long,
would take forty hours to deliver to New York or Washington,
DC, in a small rental truck.

Georgetown University professor Bruce Hoffman says that
we are as vulnerable to al-Qaeda as we were when the "war on
terrorism" commenced, judging by the number and sophistica-
tion of plots uncovered in one year (*Ottawa Citizen*, October
27, 2006). Hoffman cautions against believing "politicized intelligence" reports that al-Qaeda has been weakened since 9/11
(*Global Security Newswire*, October 27, 2006).

Not begrudging al-Qaeda a head start, fully five years passed
after 9/11 before twelve nations, led by the United States and Russia, met in Morocco to figure out how to prevent terrorists from
acquiring material for nuclear or radiological weapons (*Global
Security Newswire*, October 27, 2006). The tardiness of this exercise defies explanation. Nikolai Spassky, former deputy head of
Russia's Federal Atomic Energy Agency, asserted in 2006 that the
nonproliferation regime was in a state of crisis, citing the "unbe-
lievable growth of nuclear energy in the world," the "intellectual
atrocity" represented by the failure of the United States and Russia to agree on plans to permit Russia to import and reprocess
spent fuel that the United States has supplied around the world,
and the "serious contradiction of the failure of the Non-Proliferation Treaty" to prohibit the spread of reactor fuel production
technology (*Global Security Newswire*, October 4, 2006).

Should the president, vice president, and speaker of the
House of Representatives all be killed in a wipeout of Washington, the United States could find itself in civil war. The military would take control, but the diversity of ideology found
within the armed services, the spread of religious ideology, and
lack of political cohesion among the public, would forestall the
best efforts to call upon the nation's strengths, which are its

literacy rate, its geographical spread, and its economic strength and widely shared wealth. Our federal system would buckle. One city destroyed will leave the United States, and indeed the world, prey to a hundred forms of frenzy, panic, fears both rational and irrational, and blundering madness. If multiple cities are destroyed, the civic and cultural retrogression will be comparable, though in utterly unpredictable ways, to the Dark Ages of Europe after Rome fell.

As described in Chapter 1, dozens of indications point to awareness throughout the higher reaches of government and corporate America that we are grievously unprepared for such a catastrophe. Hurricane Katrina has served as a convenient peg on which to hang many of the crisis studies, which perhaps have hindered public awareness of the full implications of the nuclear threat. A study by the American Highway Users Alliance gave "an 'F' to 20 of the 37 largest U.S. urban areas for their capacity to evacuate residents in a crisis" (*Global Security Newswire*, October 26, 2006). The Alliance's response to its own findings was to recommend expanding highways and selling Americans more cars. And Donovan Slack of the *Boston Globe* has reported that "[t]housands of emergency gas shut-off valves—crucial safety features required by the state to stop the flow of explosive gas to homes and businesses during emergencies—are inaccessible. . . . [A]n estimated 755,000 of 1.1 million total valves across the state [Massachusetts] may have been paved over or blocked by debris or simply can't be reached" (Slack 2006).

Our Response So Far

Our vulnerability must terrify every president and ultimately every American. The terror will destabilize the nation unless steps are taken to transform the country into what most Americans want and believe it to be: a force that strives to make the world a secure place to live.

As Harvard University's Jessica Stern (2003) interviewed terrorists around the world, her subjects revealed a United States
that plays into terrorist hands by neglecting to shrink the grounds
for seeing Americans as corporate exploiters, backers of repres-
sive regimes, and consumer-driven opportunists. Reading Stern's
interviews, conducted in Pakistan, Indonesia, Israel, and other
nations, one has to believe that if the United States promoted the
enforcement of law rather than self-serving hegemony and corporate profits, fewer people would want to destroy us.

Aside from simply offering verbal constructs like "war on
terrorism," no political leader has described, and media and
publishers shield the public from discussing, initiatives to promote security based on enforced law. Such initiatives are counterintuitive to politicians' instincts to flatter voters and to avoid
suggesting that they might be obliged to accept burdens. For a
century, American politics have been molded by a preoccupation with military "solutions." Presidential elections, therefore,
the only ones most Americans take seriously, cannot be counted
on for enlightenment or progress.

Peace and disarmament advocates who were pleased to see
George W. Bush discredited over misuse of the WMD issue in
Iraq remained blinded as to the way in which he was correct,
which was the danger of nuclear proliferation and terrorism.
Peace advocates resist contemplating the steps that would be
required to employ force for arms-control enforcement, even if
that force were constrained by administrative and judicial law
enforcement organs like those that they take for granted in the
domestic realm. Experience with international economic and
trade organizations that are too heavily accountable to corporate interests has produced a low ebb of enthusiasm for global
institution-building among liberals and progressive activists. Peace advocates have never developed a comprehensive
political, legal, or institutional response to the nuclear danger.
When finally a president and Congress admitted the danger,

never mind whether the admission was sincere or an excuse for aggression, the necessary constituency for enforced universal disarmament as the alternative to the military action was nowhere to be seen. "Give peace a chance" describes a state of mind, not an action plan.

Bush did us one favor. He identified a strong element in the United States that is unlikely ever to be persuaded by reasoned discourse. Yahoos who tear about with flags fluttering from pick-up trucks today, blame martyred hero deaths on war critics tomorrow, and rally to a new war the next day must simply be taken on and outorganized and outvoted from their power bases, which include a great many city and town elective offices from which they pressure Congress and influence opinion.

Military and foreign policy experts, who might be expected to explore even far-fetched alternatives dispassionately, are too driven by short-term demands and immersed in doctrinaire policy to plan alternatives. Politicians fear getting tagged as idealists or advocates of unilateral disarmament. In many respects, even those leaders whose policy preferences are sound underrate their own constituencies' readiness for new departures. The general public (excluding the aforementioned yahoos) actually is more responsive to international solutions than the power holders allow. Benjamin Page and Marshall Boulton, in *The Foreign Policy Dis-Connect*, assert that the public "favor[s] policies amounting to something like a system of global governance to deal with a range of political, economic, and military issues. This public support does not seem to be shared, or even understood, by most U.S. foreign policy makers" (Page and Boulton 2006, 231).

Nothing short of universal arms control is faintly credible. Security based on deterrence—arming all against all—if it was ever sound, is history. To end the peril inherent in illusory security, real security must be planned in tandem with democratic control of enforcement.

International empowerment may be a last resort, but not because a superpower need not rely on collective security. And not because American singularity makes its security needs unique. It is a last resort because it is dangerous to share participation in institutions with parties that sometimes will prove hostile to the United States, and because of the inherently fractious nature of polyglot councils.

On the other hand, the idea that some nations may reliably possess WMD while others may not has been tested and proved futile. "Reliable" nations, including the United States, have facilitated proliferation even as they railed against it, selling technology that produces fissionable material, countenancing inadequate security systems and trade regulation, neglecting to prevent theft and trafficking. Allies like Pakistan, and even Germany and France, have contributed to proliferation (Langewiesche 2007). Most recently, we are told that the treaty that George W. Bush signed with India in 2006, under which a nation that declines to sign the Non-Proliferation Treaty will be assisted to create eight reactors that are not subject to IAEA inspections, carries no risk because India is "trustworthy," according to Undersecretary of State Nicholas Burns (*Global Security Newswire*, March 23, 2006).

Reliability shifts with changes in rulers, the form of government, how secure a nation feels, who its allies and opponents of the moment might be, and economic motivations. People who denigrated the Soviet Union as a viable governmental system extolled it as a reliable custodian of doomsday weapons. Then, as noted above, Russia grew dangerously porous.

In the United States, as in most countries, we leave home without weapons, accumulate possessions, pursue occupations, conduct business, express opinions, raise families, choose friends, and change governments—across lifetimes—without a thought of force or violence. Enforced law undergirds domestic social order, but when it comes to external security, to foreign relations, we extract no wisdom from domestic order and rely on firepower. If someone asserted that within our borders Americans would be safer with a military government, police at corners, and banned dissent, stability would vanish. Yet the instability of violence is our chosen global strategy. We strive for an international order of police at corners and wonder why the reaction produces terrorists.

It is futile to expect genuine peace until there is put into effect an effective system of enforceable world law in the limited field of war prevention. This implies the adoption on a world-wide basis of the measures and institutions which the experience of centuries has shown to be essential for the mainte-nance of law and order, namely, clearly stated law against violence, courts to interpret and apply that law and police to enforce it. . . .

A permanent world police force must be created and maintained which, while safeguarded with utmost care against misuse, would be fully adequate to forestall or suppress any violation of the world law against international violence.

The complete disarmament of all the nations. . . is essential, this disarmament to be accomplished in a simultaneous and proportionate manner by carefully verified stages and subject to a well-orga-nized system of inspection. . . .

Effective world machinery must be created to mitigate the vast disparities in the economic condi-tion of various regions of the world, the continuance of which tends to instability and conflict.

—from *World Peace Through World Law* by Grenville Clark and Louis B. Sohn

CHAPTER 4

My Kingdom for a Plan!
(or, The Blinders of Empire)

Though arms-control advocates warned that nuclear proliferation and terrorist possession of nuclear weapons would follow the Cold War arms race, neither of the two main political parties in the United States would offer an alternative strategy to massive nuclear arsenals. Short-term deterrence tactics always took precedence over long-term risks, no matter how predictable and extreme those risks were. Weapons construction fastened vampire-like on investment and employment interests, and were even glorified as examples of America's exceptionalism. The Soviets proved compliant competitors, either because they thought they could win the race or because they did not otherwise hope they could deter a U.S. attack.

Over the course of six decades, no one has asked how to re-achieve the minimal security of species longevity and the confidence, or faith, that no matter how painful some future decade or even century may prove, life will go on and a new era of progress will emerge. Not to imagine returning to that minimal degree of confidence in the future, not to try and guess what its components would have to be, no matter how implausible, is to give up. And our avoidance of such inquiry says to future generations, you are on your own, good luck, expect no help from us. If we continue on the present path, the hopes and opportunities that our forefathers bequeathed have been squandered. We will not pass them on.

By minimal security I mean the expectation of civilization's gradual improvement and of an orderly succession of generations in which at least some of one's grandchildren and great-grandchildren can be expected to survive, with some of the historic cities and some of the wild places intact, an expectation that even when the worst happens—war, pestilence, tyrannies— the worst will not prove terminal.

Until now it has always been possible to take humanity's future for granted. No perspective, no known facts or experience, suggested other than variations of the present as it existed from century to century. When an unfortunate group or age wondered, is this or that catastrophe the end of the world as we know it, and the catastrophe sometimes proved just that, the question pertained to the questioner's world, not to all the world, all peoples, all civilization. Until Hiroshima.

With the exhaustion of environmental resources added to the prospect of nuclear devastation, today's generation is bequeathed the prospect that it may prove to have been the piv-otal generation for eternal blame or praise. A singular honor! An honor that dictates the maximum civic effort for anyone with a sense of social obligation, whether derived from religion, ethics, affection, or sentiment.

The fault is not with technology in and of itself; technology's gifts need not end. The search for answers to the universe's mysteries is a fascinating and beneficial pursuit, and we must not keep human potential in thrall to myopic barbarity. Whatever chance our descendants get to learn where humankind's road might lead compels the here-and-now generation to pause at a way station on that road, pause long enough to jettison war. A viable future in the age of WMD necessitates that nations accept the restraint of law. Achieved now within so many nations, it undoubtedly, unquestionably, is achievable between them. The price is the political effort to wrest policy control from the war system's acolytes and dependents.

Why is discussion about concrete steps to end the threat of nuclear destruction nonexistent? Why are proposals for a staged escape not made election issues? Why have nongovernmental organizations (NGOs) and protest groups not placed a preventive strategy, in contrast with "don't do it" hand-wringing, before the public? Why does the media report on no proposals to flat-out prevent war and its modern consequences and adapt to whatever adjustments this might entail for our economies, habits, enthusiasms, and biases? Why don't my friends and I kick it around? Why is there exclusive reliance on the defensive strategies of the Department of Homeland Security, however essential cargo inspections and disaster plans have become?

By preventive strategy, I mean plans, no matter how long-term, to prevent the use of nuclear weapons, to destroy the weapons, halt manufacture, remove motivations to use them, and substitute other means for accomplishing what possessors and seekers of the weapons want to accomplish. Let us not hear that no plans are proposed because none would be practicable. Impractical plans are proposed for all kinds of endeavors. The prospect of infeasibility never stopped inventors from dreaming and imagining, and plenty of inventions owe their discovery to ideas that initially were, or seemed, infeasible. One thing leads to another—another idea, another method, another material, another supporter. Why don't we hear about cockeyed ideas to prevent nuclear destruction, given our ability to transform cockeyed into everything from can openers to the Internet?

Since World War I, we have trained and prepared almost exclusively to counter political ideologies like Communism and hostile nations like Kaiser Wilhelm's and then Hitler's Germany. We have studied religious and racial tolerance to heal our internal separations and in reaction to the Nazi Holocaust. That study has borne fruit. We Americans now must plant the seeds of that fruit.

Today's Muslim terrorism presents an amalgam of religion, political ideology, and anger. Reports about terrorists' motivations are inconsistent. We hear they are persuaded that to kill nonbelievers is their God's desire. Does that mean they aim to kill so many nonbelievers that only the faithful remain? Or that the sight of so much killing will promote adherence to rather than revulsion against their faith? Do they kill as punishment for not believing, or as punishment for actions that nonbelieving promotes or tolerates? If the latter, what are those actions—drinking, smoking, fornicating? Is it commercialism? Is it exploiting Muslims, or helping enemies of Muslims? What has captured their malevolent interest?

Do terrorists feel possessive about Middle Eastern oil reserves? Their rulers have partnered with Western capitalists for generations to exploit oil resources. What is new today? Some say they are today's resisters of modernization. Do they think economic aggression and exploitation are inherent in capitalism and free markets? Free markets connote consumer freedom of choice, but just as accurately, they mean freedom for the possessors of capital to exploit natural and human resources.

The neoconservative doctrine aimed to turn Middle Eastern countries into democracies. Does the faith in this goal suggest a belief that only the leaders of those countries are dangerous and that given a vote, the people would replace their leaders with Western-friendly leaders? Polls in fact show widespread popular sympathy with al-Qaeda.

Consider two U.S. government outreach projects—the Marshall Plan and the Peace Corps—that can claim many positive outcomes. Never mind for the moment how economic globalization destroys Third World self-sufficiency; we should consider what outreach would be appropriate and useful in lands where terrorists find their support.

Instruction may be found in efforts to prevent Iran from making enriched uranium. For Iran to create nuclear weapons would constitute a triple defeat for the United States. Iran's leaders are hostile, so it will massively arm an avowed enemy. Deterrence may not prevent Iran from surreptitiously arming terrorists and/or other nations with the weapons. Even if Iran were no more than passive or neutral toward the United States, its acquisition of nuclear arms is another retreat from the non-proliferation doctrine that the United States championed (for others) for sixty-five years. So why does the United States refrain from the requisite step of itself adhering to the doctrine, and moving toward a world free of nuclear weapons?

Despite Iran's assumed huge threat, the best the United States has come up with is "No, you won't." A huge, global threat deserves a huge, global plan, on the scale of the League of Nations, the United Nations, or the Marshall Plan. The United States, though, reacts to nuclear threats one putative enemy at a time. American leaders gave up seeking universal protection decades ago. It is as though, to prevent robberies, governments relied on jailing every potential robber instead of pursuing comprehensive protection for all robbery targets. Banks would feel vulnerable indeed if efforts to identify and arrest all the robbers before they robbed replaced safes, alarms, security guards, employee training, and police patrols.

Civic invention is shackled by the simplistic moralism of dividing people and nations into evil and good. Good people will experience rapture and the evil go to hell. India can develop nuclear weapons because it is trustworthy; Iran, North Korea, and Iraq cannot because they are evil. No American of stature any longer proposes, "Let us outlaw all such weapons," at least not in the context of an enforcement plan to accomplish such a purpose.

Philip Bobbitt comments on our state of denial: "[S]ooner or later, some non-state actor within the global network will acquire sufficient fissile material. . . . How do we think about an event that today seems at once highly unlikely and yet ultimately inevitable? How do healthy persons think about their deaths, at once so remote and yet so finally unavoidable?" (Bobbitt 2008, 476). Or, as Tolstoy put it in describing the months before Napoleon reached Moscow and the city burned:

> With the enemy's approach to Moscow, the Muscovites' view of their situation did not grow more serious but on the contrary became even more frivolous, as always happens with people who see a great danger approaching. At the approach of danger there are always two voices that speak with equal power in the human soul: one very reasonably tells a man to consider the nature of the danger and the means of escaping it; the other, still more reasonably, says that it is too depressing and painful to think of the danger, since it is not in man's power to foresee everything and avert the general course of events, and it is therefore better to disregard what is painful till it comes, and to think about what is pleasant. In solitude a man generally listens to the first voice, but in society to the second. So it was now with the inhabitants of Moscow. It was long since people had been as gay in Moscow as that year. (Tolstoy 1954, 832)

Sixty Recommendations

In 2006 the Weapons of Mass Destruction Commission, an international group convened by Sweden and chaired by Hans Blix, former director general of the International Atomic Energy Agency (IAEA), issued sixty recommendations aimed at universal, verified controls on production, trade, deployment, and use of WMD (Weapons of Mass Destruction Commission 2006). I recall that the press noted the recommendations only briefly, and that they were barely commented on by the U.S. government.

Recommendations 19 and 20 called on Russia and the United States, followed by other states, to publish their holdings of nuclear weapons and agree to move toward agreements to destroy warheads and install reliable verification of such action. Recommendations 24 through 27 called on Russia and the United States, followed by other states, to cease production of fissile weapons material, place excess materials under IAEA safeguards, and create a verification regime. Verification was thought doable and desirable; there are, in fact, rather few plants that actually produce fissile material. The United States, initially on board with this idea, "reversed its policy and declared that 'realistic, effective verification of an FMCT [fissile material cut-off treaty] is not achievable'" (Weapons of Mass Destruction Commission 2006, 104). Recommendations 28 and 29 called for a comprehensive test ban and verification, and the United States remains a nonratifier of the Comprehensive Nuclear Test Ban Treaty, contributing to the ban's not entering into force.

Recommendation 30 called for all nuclear-armed states to plan for security without such weapons, quoting President Reagan's second inaugural address: "We seek the total elimination one day of nuclear weapons from the face of the Earth." Recommendation 53 called for a more informed public debate, commending the work of Mayors for Peace and other NGOs (see Chapter 7).

This powerful summons to the threatened populations of the world cried for a means to surmount media stifling and governmental throttling. If a dozen major American cities and fifty or a hundred towns and suburbs had possessed elected officials charged to look out for opportunities to improve the security of their targeted constituents, these recommendations and the many additional recommendations respecting biological and chemical warfare threats, the role of the United Nations, and more, would have commanded an intelligible response from the White House and Congress and, at the very least, prolonged public discourse.

American unwillingness to surrender its nuclear force is the heart of the matter. The idea that international institutions might verify arms controls and keep peace meets three objections: no means exist to keep enforcement powers accountable; nondemocratic states and states hostile to the United States and its many interests, notably the commercial ones, would enjoy enhanced influence; and too many Americans are ideologically opposed to internationalism.

Americans expect deterrence to rescue them from surreptitious arsenals at the same time as they wish to appear as a formidable threat to nations whose strategy of intimidation is to demonstrate a greater willingness to sacrifice soldier lives. We do not say outright that we are unwilling to surrender our nuclear force, but we have never subscribed officially to "building down" to zero. President Obama favors reaching zero, although he says that it may not happen in his lifetime. In addition, an international Global Zero Commission has begun to meet, and has issued a four-phase plan aimed to reduce all nuclear arsenals to zero by 2030.

Too often policy-making is conceived as choosing between good and evil. We would do well to model efforts on domestic law enforcement: domestically, we do not try to separate good people from evil when deciding to whom the law applies. We impose the law on everyone, high and low, rich and poor, without regard to supposed virtue. This occurred to me on reading a *Wall Street Journal* piece by a father whose six-year-old son heard his parents discuss efforts to prevent Iran from acquiring nuclear weapons. Iran's nuclear ambitions must be prevented, Dad said, because, like the Soviet Union, it was run by evil men. Allowing for the limitations of six-year-olds, one wonders at the pea-sized vision of perpetuating an evil/good dichotomy that passes for foreign policy, instead of raising a generation that might aspire to an era of law that prevents the causes of war.

Whether speaking with a six-year-old or the president, no one will extend the hope that all evil people, to grant the columnist his terminology, will be banished from earth. If evil is here to stay, does not proliferation of numbers and destructiveness of weapons increase the likelihood of possession and use by those who intend evil? And does not our insistence on our own right to have the weapons feed the ambitions of others—evil and not—to possess them, whether because of misconceived notions about their own security or because of jealous and even irrational pride?

Analogous to the good/evil dichotomy is the dichotomy opposing democracy with nondemocracy. To say we will do business only with democracies, or that war prevention must await universal democracy, is an excuse motivated by our own distaste for rules. A *Wall Street Journal* op-ed piece by Amir Taheri (2006) lauds George W. Bush for talking tough to Iran and draws a contrast between Bush and three Democratic presidents who faced foreign policy crises. President Kennedy, Taheri notes, was willing to pay a price to end the Cuban Missile Crisis by promising not to invade Cuba and removing Jupiter missiles from Turkey. Jimmy Carter offered friendship to Ayatollah Khomeini, only to fall victim to the Iranian hostage crisis. Bill Clinton, Taheri claims, offered to recognize Iran as the Middle East's "regional power" and met rebuff. Missing from Taheri's analysis is any recognition that ad hoc hostile approaches toward nations that we cannot subjugate and could not govern seldom prove a viable solution.

Now, terrorists compound the nuclear danger. In George W. Bush's pre-9/11 months in office the prevailing strategy was to focus on state sponsors of terrorism, so the government

disregarded warnings about a terrorist attack on the grounds
that terrorism required state sponsorship. Earlier in 2001 Paul
Wolfowitz, in reference to Osama bin Laden, was quoted as saying, "He could not do all these things like the 1993 attack on
New York, not without a state sponsor" (Benjamin and Simon
2005, 144).

The Spawn of No Rules

In huge numbers, however, terrorists are spawned by the dis-
content of millions who experience a world without rules.
Many of today's discontented are Muslims (including Muslims in Europe), whose resentment is aimed especially at the
United States. In *The Next Attack*, Daniel Benjamin and Steven
Simon (2005) describe the spread of Islamization, the sense
of identity grounded in religion rather than national or ethnic
background: "The trouble, however, is that with the transnational Muslim identity comes a sense of universal grievance.
The local and the global can no longer be distinguished. Now,
the sufferings of Muslims everywhere have become even more
palpably the responsibility of every Muslim" (Benjamin and
Simon 2005, 56).

Efforts to control nuclear weapons must address such dis-
content. The clash of culture and religion entwines missile silos,
bomb factories, and terrorists. Where might discussion begin?
To what sources might we look for proposals? The Democratic
Party? Can't risk being soft. The media? Committed to the familiar. Universities? Faculties are leery of novelty. The answer is
that a few individuals, comparatively, will do it or no one will
and President Obama's initiatives surely will fail. What numbers
would be required to influence the nation's security policies? The
answer is a very few, provided that they took effective steps. In a
town of forty thousand, ten united, persistent people, over two or
three years, could prove effective. They would expand their numbers, but ten could start it. That is one in four thousand people

or, nationwide among 300 million, a total of but seventy-five thousand. Activists opposing the Iraq war can turn out two or three hundred thousand in Washington on two weeks' notice. They would be more effective in their hometowns.

While weapons control advocates were predicting vulnerability, the United States pursued missile defense—shooting missiles at other missiles—and miniaturized the weapons to the point that they no longer require missile delivery. Any of ten thousand ship containers arriving daily will serve, not to mention countless suitcases and backpacks, against which antimissile missiles, even if perfected after three decades and hundreds of billions of dollars, cannot protect us.

Global cooperation for some purposes has advanced, often facilitated by the United Nations. However, the UN is a creature of nations that guard their sovereignties to the peril of their existence. As Philippe Delmas (1997) observes in *The Rosy Future of War*, "We fail to see that the very conception of this international system dooms it to powerlessness. This is not in fact a failure but the very nature of the system. An international system based on sovereignties *cannot* be a system with real power [emphasis in original]" (Delmas 1997, 194).

The European Union promises civic evolution, but to grow from Jean Monnet's European Coal and Steel Community to the EU consumed a half century, and its security accomplishments remain limited. Witness its inability to strengthen IAEA efforts on behalf of nuclear nonproliferation, as we see in Iran, and the inability to influence events in the Caucasus region. The rest of the nations, except for an African Union that is even further from reaching effectiveness, have never begun the task of pruning the national roots of nuclear peril.

The United States betrayed its wartime and Cold War promises of leadership, preferring the dictation of empire to the dialogue of federation, and weapons superiority to weapons control. The dereliction of successive American governments in failing to pioneer enforced prohibition of WMD ultimately exposes United States urban populations to a fate that may well prove the worst that humankind has suffered since recorded history began twenty thousand years ago. Every step toward greater destructive capacity has been labeled defensive, but American cities are starkly, nakedly defenseless. Democracy was conceived as the antidote to individual hubris and greed, but most Americans have tossed aside their democratic scepters and wallow in self-absorption, where extravagance rules, and nowhere more than in weapons profiteering.

Reasoned exploration of international solutions was off the table while Republicans controlled both branches of government. Democrats have distinguished themselves as preferable only in adopting a slower pace toward Armageddon. Recent Democratic victories have owed nothing to advocacy for substituting enforced law for weapons proliferation. Those victories owe everything to a botched war and misused economy. Steps toward global control of nuclear weapons probably will not occur until history's greatest mass agony has been visited on several city populations.

Polls tell us that the American public either has not learned or has not absorbed warnings about the nuclear terrorist threat; in bypassing the issue altogether, recent presidential campaigns send much the same message. The public may be in denial, or the media and political leaders may be wary of inciting panic. Or the Homeland Security program is being insulated against doubt about its effectiveness. Or every new security initiative that occurs to anyone encounters first one and then another settled, contrary policy commitment.

If global democracy, a condition precedent to global law enforcement, cannot be made plausible in advance of the day when cities are destroyed and humanity clamors for global order, that order will be sought through tyranny. Nuclear attack, whether in war or by terrorists, will compel adoption of international safeguards through tyranny if international democracy has not evolved to the point where those safeguards can be made accountable. Today's anti-internationalists who prophesy black helicopters and world tyranny as the price of world order will be the first to champion unaccountable world order after nuclear conflagration. Because such observers view humankind as a moral hierarchy with themselves at the top, repression from above will seem more logical than universally enforced law. This is why democracy's survival depends on experimenting now with global democracy. Proven models of cross-border democracy could make tight order linked with democracy plausible in the dark days when humanity finally clamors for order.

As no foreseeable American government will attempt cross-border elections, some people somewhere who are free to experiment must leapfrog national constraints and initiate supranational order at a subnational level.

I asked [Robert] McNamara, who has come to believe that nuclear weapons should be abolished, why the United States built so many more than it realistically needed during the Cold War. "Each individual decision along the way seemed rational at the time," he told me. "But the result was insane." (Rhodes 2007, 99)

—Richard Rhodes

PART II

WHAT TO DO?

If novel, immediate, extreme action is required, what should it be? Convinced that radical international action is called for, certain that nations never will countenance such action, we access our individual resources. We ask what sort of process we might initiate to offer hope that lawful world order could be created. We start at the far end of possibility and hypothesize the "impossible"—a secure world. We identify its accountability, control of weapons, prevention of war. We acknowledge the seeming contradiction of starting at a lower-than-national level of democracy in quest of the higher-than-national level of democracy that must precede a different world order.

On June 23, 2008, the US Conference of Mayors, at its 76th annual meeting in Miami, Florida, unanimously adopted a far-reaching resolution entitled "Support for the Elimination of All Nuclear Weapons by the Year 2020."

The resolution, submitted by Mayors for Peace Vice-President Donald Plusquellic (Akron, Ohio) and 9 co-sponsors, recommends that the U.S. government "urgently consider" an agreement—the "Hiroshima-Nagasaki Protocol"—as a means of "fulfilling the promise of the NPT by the year 2020, thereby meeting the obligation found by the International Court of Justice in 1996 to 'conclude negotiations leading to nuclear disarmament in all its aspects under strict and effective international control'." (Cabasso 2008)

—2020 Vision Campaign

CHAPTER 5

Municipalities—
Soft Targets/Hard Power

Imagine a warless world. Imagine a world not at peace but in which conflict is contained, in which war between nations and whole populations is prevented, and in which weapons for war—especially nuclear weapons—are reliably prohibited. No one in history has experienced such a world, so its components must be imagined. No one will listen to a counterintuitive proposal of such huge import without being shown, as architects say, plans and specifications. Three primary components underlie this proposal:

- Law that reliably governs everywhere the manufacture, sale, and use of weapons of war, the violation of territorial integrity, human rights violations, and the exploitation of human and natural resources.

- International enforcement apparatus, including all of the means by which domestic law is enforced, meaning a regulatory administrative arm, a judicial arm, and an enforcement arm, articulated through enough regional subdivisions to embrace all peoples, empowered to compel nations, and when necessary, ungovernable subgroups, to adhere to law.

- An apparatus of democratic control that will keep the rules current and keep the enforcement apparatus accountable and therefore acceptable.

These components, with which a great many nations have been comfortable internally over hundreds of years, have been out of reach internationally due to the size and diversity of the world. Today, advanced communication and transport technologies have put the components of civic order within global, social, and political reach, provided we do not leave the initial development to the nations.

The Nation as Obstacle

Nations never will facilitate development of the three components. In the field of security, nations operate outside of law. No nation can be first to subordinate its firepower to external constraint. The United Nations cannot impose law on nations for whom it is a mere agent, possessing no independent legitimacy. The development and acceptance of security's three components must be crafted at another level of political discourse and power, by agencies working across national borders to penetrate national exclusivity in foreign policy and security matters.

Policy initiatives too radical to vet through the electoral process necessitate trial and error and time to succeed. How can those who see this start the process? Nations have proved for almost seventy years that they are incapable of treating doomsday weapons differently than crossbows, gunpowder, tanks, poison gas, and airplanes. A new weapon is always seized upon to strengthen the arsenal. National governments, left to themselves, will inevitably use a better weapon to kill more soldiers (and, increasingly, civilians) and generate more wealth. (Never forget the wealth.) Some large number of individuals therefore must reevaluate nations as the prime security bulwark. National governments cannot be left to themselves. Some number of us will have to influence events in ways that have not been tried. The only source of power to do this, surprising though it sounds, resides in the city halls and town office buildings of the world.

Although national governments remain essential at levels appropriate to the size and complexity of their populations, they conceal a double trap. Their self-glorification, preoccupation with sovereignty, unholy alliances with commercial interests, and (in many cases) holy alliances with religion incubate war. Furthermore, they are nearly useless as a political arena for inventing radical new security initiatives. No presidential aspirant can hazard a promising candidacy or a party's fortunes on unproved, much less untried, ideas.

Consider the motives that prompt the United States (like other nations) to sanction, in fact to license and promote, weapons makers to sell weapons systems around the world instead of laboring toward reduced arms levels:

1. Foreign sales reduce the unit cost of developing and manufacturing weapons that the United States itself intends to purchase.

2. Increased sales generate jobs and prosperity in every congressional district.

3. Foreign buyers grow dependent on American sources and pricing.

4. Markdowns and advanced technology reward foreign buyers for complying with U.S. strategic aims.

5. Sales that equip foreign armies cement military alliances and make those armies dependent on American suppliers for parts and replacements.

No national government will ever extricate itself from this self-defeating box. Nothing will do but for some number of individuals to create for themselves a power platform from which to study the role of arms proliferation in reducing security, devise safer security policies, and promote those policies.

The City as Solution

From 1974 to 2004, the Chicago Council on Global Affairs commissioned opinion polls that would compare public views on foreign policy goals, threats, and preferences with views of foreign policy experts in government, media, universities, and interest groups. The parallel surveys were repeated every four years. Benjamin Page and Marshall Boulton, who analyze the data in *The Foreign Policy Dis-Connect* said, "It is hard to avoid the conclusion that there has been a rather wide gulf, on many issues, between the foreign policy preferences of government officials and those of the American citizenry. Nor does the overall extent of leader-citizen disagreement appear to be related to which party controls the House and Senate, or by how big a margin" (Page and Boulton 2006, 217). They continue:

> Indeed, most Americans appear to believe in elements of what can be called "global governance": webs of international laws and institutions that serve broad U.S. interests while also furthering the interests of people worldwide and sometimes constraining the United States.... They favor a variety of diplomatic and multilateral measures to combat terrorism; express a high level of support for the United Nations; favor various concrete measures to increase the UN's capability and effectiveness; and back international treaties—several of which have been rejected by U.S. government officials—concerning the control of nuclear weapons, the prohibition of land mines, measures against global warming, and the International Criminal Court. (Page and Boulton 2006, 139)

Here is dysfunction of cosmic proportion. Populations, nations, civilization are all at stake, yet a superpower government is frozen. Cities and towns are the only political agencies through which leverage might be found. They could influence policies of their nations without subverting the nations, as individuals cannot. They are accessible political bases for individuals who lack the sponsorship of massive wealth, megamedia, or corporate power.

In finished form, global democracy is not quite imaginable. The nations would discredit any plausible model. Yet security will depend upon accountable power, without which the world will never hazard institutions equipped to prevent war. Accountability and law enforcement must evolve together. The trick must be for cross-border democracy to penetrate national boundaries while not challenging national sovereignties or compromising such security as the nations cobble together, undependable though it may be.

How to Do It

As an easy first step, elected governing bodies of a few municipalities in a half-dozen countries each might appoint one of their number to attend a security conference. They would announce that their municipal election ballots in subsequent years would include a line to elect a representative to follow-up conferences. That would break the ice. Not world government. Not pacifism. Not unilateral disarmament. Not an invasion of national sovereignty. Democracy.

A handful of citizens or organizations in any nation might write to their mayor, city council, or board of aldermen to ask for a public hearing to explore the idea. At the hearing, the municipal body would be urged to adopt a resolution that sets forth a proposed agenda for the first-year conference. (To make it easy, the appendices of this book contain suggested forms of letter, resolution, and agenda.)

Machiavelli wrote, "The ruin of states is caused... because they do not modify their institutions to suit the changes of the times. And such changes are more difficult and tardy in republics" (Machiavelli 1940, 443). In today's republics, the means for experiment are in cities and towns. Evolution beyond the nation-based UN experiment is overdue, but the American model of constitutional convention is not available. Nations and peoples are too diverse in history, practices, and capacities. Vested interests entwine the national governments, especially interests financially and emotionally committed to the war system.

On the other hand, even in authoritarian nations, municipalities possess elements of self-determination and are integral to every nation's governmental structure. They present no threat to their own or other nations. Through trade, social intercourse, art, and education, vast dialogue over borders already exists, examples of which will be discussed in subsequent chapters. In an initiative in which I participated in the mid-to-late 1980s, twenty American municipal sister city delegations dealt directly with municipal officials in the Soviet Union, America's deadly enemy, paving a way toward the Cold War thaw. Several of those relationships survived the Soviet Union's breakup (for example, the Cambridge/Yerevan and Seattle/Tashkent partnerships). Militarists and their historians attribute the Cold War thaw to America's "winning" the arms race and in the process bankrupting the Soviet Union. Never mind that the arms race hastened proliferation of nuclear weapons that jeopardize American cities today as terrorists scurry to convert the dregs of superpower arsenals into means for pounding Western civilization into shards. Never mind that the arms race fostered in our country that great compromiser of democracy, the military/industrial complex against which President Eisenhower warned.

Municipalities can knit relationships that would make the idea of international elections credible. The implications would

be shattering because the only valid obstacle to institutionaliz-
ing a means to block war is the absence of democratic accountability that must precede empowerment of such institutions.
Cross-border municipal ties would help force nations to justify
their armaments, and place a greater burden of the argument on
those who fall back on ethnic, religious, and ideological hatreds
as excuses not to institutionalize security. Citizens of authoritarian nations would find ways to influence policies of their
nations, and citizens of all governments could begin to monitor
ties between global business and governments.

No less a top dog than Defense Secretary Robert Gates has
said that to defeat terrorism, American civilians must become
involved. He spoke of "integrating" soft with hard power, a sure
way to rob soft power of its credibility, but he was on the right
track (Burns 2007).The challenge will be for participants to
maintain reciprocal credibility across the borders, for national
governments will prefer their own versions of people-to-people, sometimes well intended, sometimes merely to impose
control. Any sort of hybrid military/civilian approach was discredited in a column by William Pfaff, who said that U.S. efforts
to acquire influence over foreign policy and courts by creating
international enforcement academies in Budapest, Bangkok,
Botswana, and Costa Rica and improving the criminal justice
system "are generally regarded abroad as attempts to counter
the influence of international law and human rights NGOs, and
to oppose the UN international war crimes tribunal (Pfaff 2003).

The initiative must stay distanced from national governments and national politics. In *The Next Attack*, the authors
assert that "public diplomacy" as attempted from the American
national level has so far proved merely a "bureaucratic term for
propaganda. . . . [T]he individuals who have been given responsibility for outreach to the Muslim world have been Republican
Party stalwarts with public relations or advertising experience"
(Benjamin and Simon 2005, 218). "The administration's implicit

view of grassroots democratization programs is that they are mundane and discredited tools," say the authors, who beg to differ. "[T]he emergence of civil society is . . . the indispensable bridge between the passivity of societies shattered by political repression and the vibrant activism that begets democracy" (Benjamin and Simon 2005, 210–11).

No nation needs to sanction municipal security conferences, no threat would be posed to national sovereignties, no funds need be appropriated, no treaties signed, no constitution drafted. All that is required is for a few cities and towns in a few countries to elect representatives to formulate steps toward a security apparatus that is strong enough to police arms reductions and nuclear abolition and safe to empower. The conference needs no legal standing. The point is to gain experience with differing electoral systems, with tiers of representation that huge population numbers eventually will require, and the novel experience of representing at the same time populations, municipalities, regions, and nations (their peoples, not their governments). Over a decade, the body would acquire institutional wisdom and develop precedent. It would address the security aspects of racial, religious, ethnic, and class preoccupations. It would unite people. It would advise the United Nations and, depending on the confidence accrued, ultimately subsume portions of the UN's jurisdiction.

The trick is to build in increments, thus inventing global democracy as we go along. No element of existing security systems needs to be replaced until a better element is available. The goal would be accountable enforcement that protects rather than encroaches upon national sovereignties. Six decades brought us to the moment on 9/11 when terrorism and national vulnerability were conjoined. This is a hole that we might be able to get out of in another five or six decades— not much quicker, but with greater certainty than attends such security measures, necessary though some of them may be, as screening imports; dictating to other peoples when we consider their regimes intolerable; and trying to convince Iran, North Korea, and Syria that we could determine after a terrorist attack where nuclear bomb components originated.

Anyone who protests that there is no time to create such an unprecedented system must ask themselves if they can imagine a secure world in which weapons production, marketing, and use are not reliably regulated. Can anyone imagine achieving security without universal rule-making and rule enforcement, or without peace enforcement constraints? Can nations scale down armed forces absent a reliable shield against aggression?

These questions do not promote an impossible agenda. They promote an agenda that ultimately will prove inconsistent with both the international arms bazaar and any one nation's possession of excessive power. They are posed to urge that arms-control advocates, as citizens and therefore power holders in the urban terror targets, initiate a radical but feasible first step—radical not in difficulty or strangeness, but only as an unfamiliar application of commonplace practices.

Fifty years ago C. Wright Mills insisted that politics must address the necessity for a "wilful making of history" (Mills 1960, 115). He told intellectuals to "propose new terms for the world encounter" (Mills 1960, 153).

> The root error of judgment involved is the insistence that any vision, demand, hope must be such as to be immediately realizable this week, or at furthest by the next election. If this insistence is dogmatic, as it usually is nowadays, then all political thinking is simply stopped. It is replaced by mere calculations of clique and party strategy. (Mills 1960, 115)

Public awareness that elected representatives from many cities are engaged across borders to seek authentic security will have instant impact. Even if two decades of trial and error must attend exploratory learning and implementation, the evident determination by increasing numbers to work across borders in a civic and governmental context (as distinguished from arming and manipulating on the one hand, and marching and protesting on the other) would start to dissolve cynicism and discredit exploitation. It would rejuvenate elections and help make the case for democracy's evolutionary capacity. The lure of terrorism would diminish.

People feel uninformed and wary of divisive issues. Some might think that to meld local with global would magnify the prejudice and confusion that blight international relations. Some might argue that local voices will prove so influential as to tie a president's hands in diplomacy and security strategy: foreign countries will play off Americans against one another, and American promises and threats will grow undependable. In fact, though, America will begin to speak in a more united and authentic way. Vociferous testing of public policy validates majority decisions. Greater proximity of people to the issues and decisions that will determine their fate will discredit policies that pander to a few, reward friends, and inflame passions.

Populations targeted in their homes for mass slaughter are today bystanders. Among those of us fortunate enough to avoid immediate peril, too few follow, discuss, or influence the policies that will endanger us or keep us safe. To draw issues into the local arena would be a step toward reducing them to democratic control. Matters that are captive to ideologies or economic interests, or are too novel or politically dangerous to influence through presidential or congressional elections or by lobbying, will become what they should be: stimulants for creative thinking and beneficiaries of sound analysis.

To define security and other global issues, such as the environment and economic stability, as local issues would invigorate the public. Instead of waiting sheep-like for Armageddon, people would rise to necessity and make feasible what is held to be impossible. Machiavelli cites "the diversity of the genius of her citizens" as the resource of republics that "enables the republic better to accommodate herself to the changes of the times than can be done by the prince" (Machiavelli 1940, 442).

To shield city dwellers from the issue of their own security reflects little confidence in democracy. If one relies on democracy to achieve a stable, prosperous society, as Americans do, one must believe that people have the intelligence and civic conscience to cast objective, reasoned votes. One must believe that they will obtain the information they need, reflect on it, discuss options, and draw conclusions.

Discouraged by seeming complexities, we allocate less and less time to what is most important. Less reliance is placed on putting citizens in charge and capitalizing on their reason and wisdom. Low voter turnouts, uncontested elections, demagoguery, mendacity, and crippled discourse all speak to democracy's narrowing scope. The enthusiasm attending the 2008 presidential election, while heartening, ought not be counted on as evidencing a trend, considering the degree of trouble into which George W. Bush got the country, the very limited specifics regarding security that the Democratic contender offered us, and the fact that presidential politics, at best, merely scratch the surface of public engagement.

To invest local representatives with international responsibility would help end the disconnect between what we think of as local issues, like schools, housing, police, sanitation, land conservation, and the global issues of war, climate change, and economic disparities. To meld local and national at the points where they necessarily connect would repair our fractured hold on what imperils us.

Cities and towns might incubate a generation responsible and informed enough to gain control over its future. If children saw their parents treating security as something for which the parents were responsible, they would prepare themselves to do the same. The only place where children can learn to distinguish the important from the trivial is the community in which they live.

Cities and towns may be the last hope for fading democracy. Civic maturity and confidence in democracy necessitate authentic communication, understanding, persuasion, toleration, and consensus molding, all of which have to be experienced in schools, around the dinner table, and over the back fence. Private discussion has to precede public discussion. Democracy is nothing, though, until the individual achieves a public voice, for instance by access to local media. Democratic government needs training grounds for political awareness, leadership, and discipline. Moreover, cities and towns would serve as megaphones for individuals and private groups seeking to lobby Washington.

If, as political scientists maintain, American states serve as laboratories where novel policies and programs can be tested without putting the nation at risk, what about municipal initiatives? Who would claim that our national government successfully interacts with the Muslim world? Would anyone deny there are millions of Americans, including many Muslims, who would do anything to prevent nuclear terrorist attacks and could with the right opportunity show a friendly countenance to Muslims everywhere?

Citizens aggregated through their cities and towns might do for democracy what corporations did for business. The modern corporate form, barely a century old, organized, focused, and magnified individual capacities. Stock ownership collected and directed wealth. Management organized talents. Corporations employed the economies of mass resource exploitation and marketing. Heralded as the apotheosis of economic freedom, capitalism more accurately is the triumph of organized aspirations, abilities, and needs.

Through an analogous revolution, municipal corporations (the legal term for cities) might act to empower fragmented, manipulated, and powerless individuals by providing the essentials of effective citizenship. Those essentials are a forum for debate, education, talent recruitment, vote assembling, lobbying, leadership structure, and power exercise. Individuals will enjoy greater incentive to be informed and exercise judgment when they possess a political arm small enough to have a personal hand in directing, while large enough, in concert with other municipalities, to influence state and national policies, and by crossing borders, the world. War that now is irrationally touted by its devotees as either a regrettable expression of human nature or man's highest expression of civic devotion might yet join cattle rustling as the stuff of novels instead of a universal calamity of species-threatening dimensions.

National plans to avoid nuclear catastrophe remain mired in strategies for winning wars, though nuclear war cannot be won and nuclear terrorism has nothing to do with war. Consider the utter failure of nations to eliminate the causes of war and terrorism, including but not limited to arms races, unstable ethnic and religious competitions, threatening alliances, economic disparities, corporate exploitation, the absence of effort to strengthen the war prevention and peacekeeping capacities of the UN—all rarely addressed by national governments and never addressed effectively.

National elections do not formulate matters so as to inform multitudes or stimulate debates through which people might reason together, reach conclusions, and authorize action. The way that national elections are run, information is not provided, dialogue not fostered, consensus building avoided, majority decisions fabricated and illusory. It takes a train wreck like the recent Bush administration to stimulate the outpouring of effort that should attend every election. Even 2008's massive public engagement fell short of promoting searching dialogue about the supreme issue of security.

Why do governments rely so heavily on unilateral national military solutions? Is leadership training so limited that the heads of state cannot think strategically in international law and politics? Do generals command the diplomats? Do arms makers confer the power? If the United Nations were democratized through international elections, might it grow accountable enough to safely command the force required to enforce peace? National dialogue about such matters is not attempted because the present military-based security system is seldom questioned, inadequate though the system has been since Hiroshima, and discredited as it ought to be since September 11, 2001.

The defects of democracy as practiced here and abroad will be cited as reasons why democratizing security issues cannot work. Low voter turnout, deteriorating quality of media presentation, and citizen apathy and passivity all suggest that the enlargement of democracy is doomed to failure. Let us remember, though, that (a) people do respond when they think they can be effective and when the outcome will have a strong impact on their personal interests, as the 2008 election showed; (b) while one hopes for large-scale participation, the immediate aim is simply to invent a counterweight to the self-interested controllers of security policies, and for this any substantial block of urban voters will suffice; (c) an idea conceived in the throes of desperation deserves tolerance—show me, I say, why we should not feel desperate over the danger of nuclear armed terrorists, after George Tenet and so many others who should know tell us they feel desperate; and (d) hostility to the U.N. promoted by conservative anti-internationalists and swelling corporate global power dictate experimenting with global citizen empowerment.

CHAPTER 6

Common Cause: Why Should Cities Cooperate? The Argument

Surprising numbers do not want to feel that the human race is experiencing a security crisis. Somehow doing so would undermine too much of their chauvinism that denigrates other people's values and allegiances, whether religion, nation, race, economic system, or simply way of life. They prefer to see others, in whatever category they place others, as competitors for a place in the sun. Their own worth somehow depends on belittling the worth of others. One can only hope that World War III or the terrorist destruction of cities are not requisite to a general awareness that in the nuclear age, security is a precondition for the longevity of any and all values.

Nations are composed of communities. As communities do not negotiate with nations other than their own, so nations do not communicate with other nations' communities. The U.S. State Department cannot make common cause with the citizens of Afghanistan, Iraq, Iran, and North Korea, where so many live who hate Americans. But Scranton, Pennsylvania, can. American cities and towns can make common cause for survival with citizens of other countries, basing initiatives on similar employment, immigration history, cultural interests, sports, leisure activities, or just a shared sense of peril. If Americans are broiled under a mushroom cloud, let it not be for lack of efforts to have reached the neighbors and families of their terrorist attackers, or to deal personally with people who have built the weapons.

John Brady Kiesling wrote *Diplomacy Lessons: Realism for an Unloved Superpower* after he resigned from the Foreign Service in 2003 because his conscience could not accommodate the Iraq invasion. Serving in embassies in Israel, Greece, Armenia, Morocco, and at the State Department's Romania and India desks, he had long pondered how the United States could influence other nations. The first reality, he says, is that any would-be influencer starts as an outsider in a world that all nations separate into insiders and outsiders.

Put another way, Kiesling says, sovereignty is every nation's crown jewel. The would-be influencer must respect that jewel by acquiring, and helping national leaders one wishes to influence to acquire, "transnational legitimacy" (Kiesling 2006, 44). National leaders rarely enjoy sufficient legitimacy with their own constituencies and are in no position to yield any part of the national dignity to an outside power. "A key aim of U.S. foreign policy," Kiesling concludes, "must be to reinforce the legitimacy of foreign politicians so that they will be secure enough domestically to ignore the political costs of doing what America demands. Legitimacy would be a miraculous gift if America had it to bestow.... Unfortunately, there is no such source of American transnational legitimacy" (Kiesling 2006, 43–44).

Here in a nutshell is why security cannot be left to individual nations or alliances of nations. Only international law, enforced, can produce transnational legitimacy. The price of law is to bind all parties. However, American leaders, as superpower wielders, too often become toadies for commercial interests and dependent on pumped-up patriotism. They cannot risk being bound. Hence superpower impairs security where it ought to enhance it. The nation whose support for international law is indispensable does not support it. The result is the perpetuation of a lawless world in the face of terminal weapons.

Kiesling recounts the failed American efforts to forestall India's nuclear weapons tests that invited Pakistan's pursuit of nuclear capability and weakened the Non-Proliferation Treaty. Indians, he says, have a "sense of superior morality" that could be mined productively in diplomacy by agencies that did not suffer from American moral deficiencies (Kiesling 2006, 228). While he does not suggest public diplomacy as proposed in these chapters, non-national, citizen-based agencies would seem the logical means for reaching out to population groups divided by dissension within other nations.

One nation meddling in the affairs of another sets population components against each other, which invites civil war. The size, complexity, and multitude of interests that compose the United States complicate policy formation and execution. However, this very size, complexity, and multiplicity offers Americans ways to engage other populations on numerous levels, more realistically and sincerely.

Municipal security undertakings would provide a common-cause outlet for diverse groups. Cities interacting over national borders in a common search for security would be able to lay the groundwork for productive dialogue within conflict-riven countries. The meeting of Sunnis and Shiites, Muslims and Christians outside their own nations with the purpose

of strengthening the security of their home cities would provide
things to think about aside from local rivalries.

National policy suffers multiple distortions: the personal
influence of friends of presidents and other powerful Americans (for example, the Saudi friends of the Bushes); the political
handicaps of presidents and the party in power (for example, a
weakened Clinton's reluctance to deal forcefully with the Afghan
al-Qaeda training camps); the immunity of religious groups
from political interference (for example, the Saudi mission-
ary program that constructed fifteen hundred mosques around
the world); and national reliance on clandestine intelligence,
such as that which, Kiesling says, "betrayed America in Iraq and
will always betray the superpower—and not only because it is
wrong—because it illuminates only a small part of a much larger
picture of how the world operates" (Kiesling 2006, 262).

I address elsewhere some of the objections to this line of
thinking, notably the associated beliefs that aggressive human
nature condemns us to wage war, and that war refreshes a
nation's spiritual health, robustness, and sense of identity. I also
have said that it would be premature to try to invent details
ahead of experience and experimentation. Here I shall, briefly,
respond to a few more of the probable objections.

One problem will be national governments trying to use
the municipal forums for their own purposes by manipulating the municipal security representative elections, discrediting positions inconsistent with national policy, and intimidating
the elected representatives. Careful international monitoring
of elections in emerging and otherwise questionable democracies may mitigate some of these obstacles. Former president
Carter has headed several key election-monitoring projects,
and credentialing is a key step preceding the Democratic and
Republican presidential nominating conventions. The municipal security conferences will develop their own system. Experiments in cross-border democracy (which might expand, as

suggested in Chapter 14, to include representative districts embracing parts of more than one nation) will link the security deficit with issues relative to the environment, economic stabilization, racial and gender justice, and so on.

How do I value the world's diverse populations? Who beyond family and friends is precious to me? Fellow residents of my town? Other Americans? Europeans? Africans? Do some groups have greater value to me than others, and do larger groups have more value than smaller ones? What is culture worth, or religion? Is distance a negative value, the value of not threatening me, not falling into some large-scale horror that disquiets me? Do I reevaluate if I perceive that my compatriots and I are hostage to the security of another people? If the safety of populations has become, or may become, compromised by nondeterrable nuclear terrorists, these are fair questions along the way to deciding to which extremes of invention the search for security might lead me. Must all violence somehow be constrained, or can constraints exempt the subnational level? Any thought that war's violence can be restricted to armies became history centuries ago. If all are hostage to all, law's restraint on war must be universal.

It is curious that we face apocalypse and imagine that an army brandishing apocalyptic weapons might prevent it. We suppose apocalypse can be one-way and imposed by the first to act. In fact, civic—not military—invention is called for. The invention doubtless must evoke force, hopefully in diminishing degrees as legal modes of organization replace military modes. And law's force must be controlled by collective hands, not one superpower. "Superpower" armies must be recognized as adjuncts to apocalypse, agents for universal ruin.

The public's exposure to nuclear terrorism is the extreme, even logical, conclusion of the consignment to victimhood that nations have accorded populations for a long time, since the French Revolution according to David Bell. In *The First Total*

War Bell concludes that French philosophers "transformed peace from a moral imperative into a historical one. . . . [T]hey opened the door to the idea that in the name of future peace, any and all means might be justified—including even exterminatory war" (Bell 2007, 77).

Instead of agreeing that our superpower strength should be directed toward creating a peaceful world, Bell observes, Americans dismiss one another as either delusional doves or paranoid, war-mongering hawks: "There has been a recurrent and powerful tendency to characterize the conflicts that do arise as apocalyptic struggles that must be fought until the complete destruction of the enemy and that might have a purifying, even redemptive, effect on the participants. . . . [Thus] the dream of perpetual peace and the nightmare of total war have been bound together in complex and disturbing ways, each sustaining the other" (Bell 2007, 3).

War is not only *not* the route to future peace, it is not the appropriate response to terrorism. It no longer should be seen as an instrument of statecraft at all, because its horror has grown unbounded and uncontrollable, engulfing whole populations. This expansion has occurred in direct relation to increasing firepower, from stirrups and steel and gunpowder to poison gas, airplanes, and atomic bombs. Nazi genocide, fire bombing, nuclear bombing—each new invention saw the nations' capacity to slaughter joined by the willingness to visit the most extreme punishments on civilians.

As the ultimate object of value, people must recoup some of the power that they trustingly deposited with national governments. As the public's agents for dealing with the rest of the world, national governments are failing, directing vast destructive powers against other peoples, not just armies, that cannot but produce retaliation in kind. And the government's power to protect recedes still more with the expansion of global corporate power, short both on compassion and accountability.

In fact, government capacity to act with constructive and benign motives seems to have contracted just as its capacity for maximum cruelty has enlarged. It was assumed that America's federal government would speak for the diverse interests of the states and the public. The public's ultimate interest, though, is security. The moment security grows doubtful, national credibility and usefulness shrinks. American citizens now must summon their wits for a personal confrontation with foreign affairs.

Hitler's Stuka squadrons dive-bombing Poland in the beginning of World War II; his indiscriminate bombing of London, including the first missiles; the Allied fire bombing of Dresden, Tokyo, and many other targets; and the destruction of Hiroshima and Nagasaki, which was intended, it turns out, to intimidate the Soviet Union rather than defeat already defeated Japan (Alperovitz 1995) should have prompted nations after the war to organize dependable protection of populations. No value could have been greater than to ensure populations against again being served up for mass sacrifice in the coliseum of advanced weaponry.

Nations should have deprived themselves long ago of ever-more-ruthless armies, especially as the armies are more ruthless not so much due to hateful, cruel, or destructive desire but to the logic and momentum of competition, profits, and technical achievement outpacing civic invention. The means to prevent or at least control military invention, production, and deployment were always within our reach, but arms competition was preferred. The UN was left dependent on the good nature of nations, an unarmed handmaiden of their diplomacy. The ultimate value, humankind's security, was left unattended.

Human fortunes and prospects have been wagered for sixty-five years upon a single slot on history's roulette wheel—deterrence, but deterrence cannot foil suicidal terrorists. The failure has been a direct result of ever greater reliance on military power. Confronted with overwhelming force, the infinitely resourceful human mind counters with the suicide bomber. Against the approaching day of the nuclear-armed suicide bomber, after sixty-five years and trillions of dollars, deterrence is as outdated as a musket.

Terrorists, it would seem, do not find their self-worth or their sense of completeness from membership in the same kind of society as I do. I am content to work and carry on family, community, and civic life in my nation of birth and community of choice because these places constitute the life that I value and enjoy. Terrorists seem to lack corresponding feelings about their places of birth and residence. They seek personal fulfill-ment by destroying what fulfills me. I do not comprehend why destroying me should fulfill them. There is talk about revenge for what my nation has done. There is talk about enabling their God to triumph by destroying those who do not believe in Him. Whatever it is, it is today's world, today's reality, and I must learn it. I cannot say to myself as it seems that America's politi-cal right wing says: "Let the world change, I will never change."

Surely we can distinguish accommodation to evil from out-witting evil. If my nation cannot defend me against suicide bombers, I must find, or create, an alternative defense. Part of suicide bombers' resourceful defense against armies has been to find self-worth in an alternative calculation. If I want to reach suicide bombers in order to defend everything I value, I must achieve some recalculation of my own. As terrorists all reside in communities, my municipality may prove a better agency than my nation to search for terrorist motives and intentions. If I want to meet the Glory Seeker where he lives, I need the keys to his city, and as a step in that direction, I write a letter to the mayor of my own city.

CHAPTER 7

Federalism— Familiar, Trustworthy, Layered Government: Reclaim the Local Level

Municipal ballots that elect an international security congress will pour foundations for two pillars of a secure world. The first pillar is cross-border democracy, and the second is expanded federalism. The two are interdependent: the power to regulate arms manufacture and trade and to prohibit aggression and the mistreatment of populations cannot and should not be assembled absent the means to hold it accountable.

The classic proposal to obtain accountability through global democracy, first published in 1958, is *World Peace Through World Law* by Grenville Clark and Louis B. Sohn. Clark and Sohn proposed transforming the UN General Assembly into a 744-member elected body whose voting power would be proportional to national populations. Following a 1982 proposal by Jeffrey Segall, a major step in the Clark/Sohn direction was taken when more than a hundred NGOs formed the International Network for a UN Second Assembly (INFUSA). It advocated an elected advisory assembly that would represent the "world's public" and assist NGOs to make their views known to the General Assembly. Each UN member nation was to choose its own method of electing representatives, the number of whom would be proportional to the nation's population, producing a body of about 550 members. INFUSA held annual conferences through 1995.

Certain observers think that the way around the violence-dependent nation structure is through NGOs. Elise Boulding points to "eighteen thousand transnational bodies (NGOs)" (Boulding 1993, 167) that facilitate citizen participation. Many of these organizations were expressly formed to promote peace and prevent war, and such groups represent immense numbers of individuals performing important work. In 1995 *Our Global Neighborhood: Report of the Commission on Global Governance* proposed that an annual Forum of Civil Society, consisting of representatives of three hundred to six hundred UN-accredited civil society organizations, be convened as an evolutionary step, to be succeeded in time by an assembly of parliamentarians (Commission on Global Governance 1995, 258).

In his essay "United Nations: Prince and Citizen?" Marc Nerfin notes that UN agencies like the International Labour Organization (ILO) and the United Nations Educational, Scientific and Cultural Organization (UNESCO) are composed, in part, of NGOs and board members who act individually rather than as state representatives (Nerfin 1993, 153). World assemblies and conferences draw individuals, organizations, and national representatives to study and recommend action on supranational issues. Mikhail Gorbachev proposed forming consultative councils, a global body under UN sponsorship, and regional councils of prominent scientists, public officials, writers and musicians,

Nobel Prize winners, religious leaders, and so forth. They would have no governmental duties. He called them a "worldwide brain trust" and a "council of the wise" (Gorbachev 2000, 230). The European Union, through which member states send popularly elected representatives to the European Parliament, is the most ambitious transfer of segments of national sovereignty to a collective effort. The lack is not models, but the mechanics to enlist enough power seekers and power holders to command ballot access in multiple languages.

Much peace-oriented NGO work is accomplished by or through local governments. In the early 1980s the Nuclear Weapons Freeze Campaign persuaded 769 U.S. city councils, county councils, and town meetings to pass nuclear freeze resolutions (Alger 1993, 261). Fifty cities and counties passed freeze votes by popular referenda, and 154 cities supported a comprehensive nuclear test ban. Nuclear-Free America reported in July 1989 that 4,279 communities in twenty-three countries had declared themselves nuclear-free zones. These steps have served the growing instinct that people must free themselves from regimentation on behalf of nationalistic programs.

Chadwick Alger quotes Jane Jacobs, David Harvey, Manuel Castells, Rajni Kothari, and others who have commented, in various contexts, that municipalities have both economic and security reasons to free themselves to a degree from their national governments and cooperate across national boundaries (Alger 1993, 264–70). Alger also quotes Robert Dahl and Edward Tufte (1973):

> Rather than conceiving of democracy as located in a particular kind of inclusive, sovereign unit, we must learn to conceive of democracy spreading through a set of interrelated political systems. . . . The central theoretical problem is no longer to find suitable rules, like the majority principle, to apply within a sovereign unit, but to find suitable rules to

apply among a variety of units, none of which is sovereign.
(Dahl and Tufte 1973, 135)

Richard Falk, though, in "Nuclear Weapons and the Renewal
of Democracy," regrets the "political futility that confronts a
peace-minded citizenry" (Falk 1986, 483). Despite the popular
consensus in the advanced industrial world that nuclear weapons should have no purpose beyond serving as the ultimate
deterrent against nuclear blackmail or attack, Democratic and
Republican leaders alike have been willing to "accept a wider
role for nuclear weapons, including their use of the weapons
to deter certain nonnuclear attacks and their use as threats
to achieve diplomatic results; it includes also at the least, the
development of nuclear war fighting capabilities and contingency plans for winning nuclear wars of different scopes" (Falk
1986, 438).

The futility of waiting for national governments to apply
common sense to the nuclear danger, Falk says, is a product
of the declining effectiveness of representative government. "It
is essential that political energy flow upward and that leaders
remain accountable to the people" (Falk 1986, 439). He does
not mean that the citizenry of various countries are always of a
peaceful mind or that they cannot be worked up to favor state
violence. The opportunity must exist, however, for the peace-
minded to influence their fellow citizens and, if successful, to
move state policy.

The untaken step is to institutionalize an elective body ded-
icated to security that prohibits force.

Robert D. Putnam (1993) chose Italy's 1970 regional decentralization to study how populations with contrasting social
histories fared over a twenty-year period when provided new
opportunities to shape their destinies. Power over municipal
government, agriculture, housing, health services, public works,
and economic development had been delegated to twenty

elected regional councils. Putnam concluded that, although initially disabled by partisan disagreement, "the new institution witnessed a steady, powerful centripetal tendency in regional politics. As ideological distances narrowed, tolerance across party lines blossomed" (Putnam 1993, 29).

Putnam says, "Regional politicians no longer see their world in stark blacks and whites, but in more nuanced (and more negotiable) shades of gray" (Putnam 1993, 33) and this despite surveys that showed that during the same twenty years, "partisan hostility was actually on the increase among ordinary Italian voters" (Putnam 1993, 29). Regional politicians who were in power before and after the changes became more responsible, and a new cadre of politicians appeared. Putnam measured indicators of institutional performance, including cabinet stability, budget promptness, innovative legislation, health expenditures, housing, and citizen satisfaction. The highest performance scores occurred in the more well-to-do northern regions, where a history of productive civic association and engagement went back to the Middle Ages. However, "in both South and North, the new institution nurtured a more moderate, pragmatic, tolerant elite political culture. In both South and North, the reform altered old patterns of power and produced more genuine subnational autonomy than unified Italy had ever known" (Putnam 1993, 30).

What assurance does a study like Putnam's hold for ending war? Allow for Italy's twenty regions speaking a common language, but consider as well the huge disparity that Putnam discovered in what the northern and southern regions brought to the task. That the rural southern regions should have benefited least is less significant than that industrially advanced areas, most similar to American states, did much better. We must conclude that delegation of some responsibility for the world's salvation to cities and towns would produce an outpouring of civic energy.

The trick is to frame the assignment as "What can we do to help?" instead of the way that anti-internationalists usually frame it: "What are those foreigners trying to get from us now?" The George W. Bush administration's putative goal of bringing democracy to Iraq may have proved as persuasive to Americans at the start of the Iraq War as the stated goal of taking away Saddam's WMD. Whether the former goal was conceived and communicated as dishonestly as the latter I leave to the reader's judgment, but the public's response speaks to a generosity that is available for war prevention if Americans were weaned from trying to express the country's principles through militarism.

Never has the need been greater to experiment with expanded federalism. Whether to rescue nation states from nuclear disaster or to avoid the supranational police state that will follow such a disaster, let us find how to break the eternal cycle of war.

Cross-border elections that must precede a global security system can be achieved initially only through the municipal level of the federal system. Such elections will prove the building blocks of accountability and control for the international administrative, judicial, and enforcement agencies that must prevent war. Democracy must accompany empowerment. It would be futile and dangerous to draft a "constitution" setting up a preconceived security apparatus empowered to make disarmament inspections, invade noncomplying nations, and adjudicate disputes. The institutions must emerge by degrees, calibrated by experiments with cross-border elections, elections that could begin next year in a hundred cities and towns, electing delegates authorized to start pitching security bridges across cultural and historical divides.

As no element of the present security system, ineffective though it is, can be surrendered until a corresponding safer element is prepared to take over, the transition must be gradual and experimental. Issues apart from security—environmental, social, economic—cry as well for the empowerment of account-able global institutions, but the initial focus should address the greatest risk. Essential institutions for the overlapping crises will develop on parallel, converging paths. The challenge is to resist efforts of the manipulators, the riggers, the puppeteers of wealth, hate, and violence to discredit transnational experi-ments with peoples, communities, and elections by branding them "world government."

Consider the wealth of existing models and patterns of supranational and subnational organization. Gary Marks and Liesbet Hooghe (2004), in "Contrasting Visions of Multi-Level Governance," identify two kinds of federalism; the first, employed in the United States and European Union, establishes a tier of discrete jurisdictions, territorial and nonintersect-ing at each level. The second is task-specific, often not related to geographic affinity. Examples include alliances convened to support ozone layer protection, facilitate hazardous waste ship-ment, and promote migratory fowl conservation. Many of these endeavors are private-public partnerships and thrive partic-ularly well in border regions. The authors, in a 2002 survey of American metropolitan areas, counted over thirty-five thousand such groups devoted to purposes like fire protection, cemeter-ies, libraries, parks, highways, airports, energy supply, and tran-sit, to give but a few examples. This number has approximately tripled over the course of fifty years.

Real-World Federalism Examples

The U.S. Constitution was created from whole cloth at a con-vention lasting just 115 days. The states enacted fifty variations on the theme, not to mention thousands of local and munic-ipal democratically elected governments, with an array of city councils, boards of aldermen, town meetings, selectmen, may-ors, and managers. America's layered system of government—national, state, and municipal—offers separate and overlapping vehicles for citizen initiative and innovation. Americans, of all people, should appreciate federalism's power and versatility.

During the Great Depression of the 1930s, a public works program, the Public Works Administration (PWA), and an employment program, the Works Progress Administration (WPA), provided federal funds that were administered at the state and municipal levels to create employment for a country out of work. The revitalization of cities was sparked by Great Society programs in the 1960s that funneled federal tax resources to municipalities for housing, business districts, cultural projects, and transportation systems. Today federal funding empowers and enables state and municipal governments, all answerable to the electorate, in dozens of fields, like education, health, and housing. As these pages go to press, the government is preparing another generation of economic-stimulation measures that once again will capitalize on federalism's adaptability.

The civil rights movement was played out between the national government and citizens at the municipal level, who managed during several crucial years to maneuver around the obstacles created by segregationist state governments. Harvard professor Archon Fung (2004), in *Empowered Participation: Reinventing Urban Democracy,* describes how Chicago decentralized school and police administration, enlisting thousands of citizens empowered by special training in hundreds of local school councils and comparable police bodies.

The Bush administration rejected the 1997 Kyoto Protocol, but American cities went to work to compensate for their nation's shirking of planetary responsibility for the environment. In a *Boston Globe* article published August 13, 2006, Juliet Eilperin reported:

> With federal lawmakers deadlocked on how best to curb global warming, state and local officials across the country are adopting ambitious policies and forming international

alliances aimed at reducing greenhouse gases.... This month former president Bill Clinton launched an effort with 22 of the world's largest cities to cut their emissions.... Recently, 22 states and the District of Columbia have set standards demanding that utilities generate a specific amount of energy—in some cases, as high as 33 percent—from renewable sources by 2020.... "Like most mayors, I'm disappointed the federal government has not taken more of a lead on this issue, but so be it. We're moving forward," said Albuquerque's mayor, Martin J. Chavez. (Eilperin 2006)

In the same issue of the *Globe*, Peter Slevin reports on the seventeen-year effort by Mayor Richard M. Daley of Chicago to exercise municipal policy to affect global warming:

There are 2.5 million square feet of green roofs completed or under construction, boosted by expedited permitting and density bonuses for developers.... [O]ther cities have climbed on board.... The urban environmental movement has spread from the margins to the mainstream, from a countercultural statement... to a policy option welcomed in boardrooms and council chambers. (Slevin 2006)

Jim Carlton, in the February 11, 2008, *Wall Street Journal* article "Nine Cities, Nine Ideas," summarized "a world-wide movement by cities to rein in their runaway energy use" (Carlton 2008). Seven hundred American mayors have signed an agreement to follow the Kyoto Protocol. Chicago's green roof program has increased in size to four million square feet and the city began to replace alley pavements with porous material that allows water to penetrate the soil (Saulny 2007). New York is experimenting with tide-driven electric generators and will require taxis to switch to hybrid fuel technology (Hanley 2007). Thane, India reduces property taxes 100 percent for buildings with solar water heaters. London plans to obtain electric power from local sources, reduce dependence on the national grid, and reduce transmission losses.

Los Angeles committed to the Kyoto targets soon after Antonio Villaraigosa was reelected mayor in 2005; the city is shooting for generation of 20 percent of its energy from renewable sources by 2010 and 35 percent by 2020. Sixteen thousand diesel trucks will be off the road by 2012. Cambridge, Massachusetts, "seeking to become the greenest city in the country," has undertaken to conserve energy in every building in the city (*Boston Globe*, March 29, 2007). All 23,000 buildings will receive energy audits over a five-year period, and property owners will be offered low- or zero-interest loans for remediation. In November 2007, nine Midwestern governors and the premier of Manitoba signed an agreement to reduce carbon emissions based on several American interstate, regional pacts (Broder 2007).

At the December 2007 UN Climate Change Conference in Bali, New York City mayor Michael Bloomberg said that mayors "are the ones who are held accountable to their public every day on a wide range of issues. . . so cities should have greater say, because they are the ones who will have to do the work." Al Gore asserted, "My own country, the United States, is principally responsible for obstructing progress here in Bali." Parallel perspectives would not be off the mark as to security from WMD disaster, whose threat is as logically predictable, even if less measurable, than climate change. Chief UN climate scientist Rafenda Pachauri said that the 2008 U.S. presidential election or the "combined actions of states and cities" might alter the U.S. approach to climate change (Hanley 2007).

Cities and towns have long experience in internationalism. A security congress will be novel only in its insistence that nations have failed to aspire high enough on the scale of necessities. That the aspiration is overdue is obvious from reading President Dwight D. Eisenhower's admonition in 1956 to a nascent program called People to People International: "If we are going to take advantage of the assumption that all people want peace, then the problem is for people to get together and to leap governments—if necessary to evade governments—to work out not one method but thousands of methods by which people can gradually learn a little bit more of each other" (Eisenhower 1956, 750). People to People International led to the creation of Sister Cities International (SCI) in 1967. According to a July 11, 2006, news release of the United States Information Program, 2,500 communities in 134 countries participate in sister cities programs. More than one thousand U.S. cities have foreign partners.

Cities have not been shy about pairing with foreign communities even when not initially countenanced by the mainstream SCI. As noted earlier, during the Cold War, twenty U.S. cities twinned with Soviet cities on the grounds of mutual security. After the breakup of the Soviet Union, most of these relationships entered the SCI tent. Still outside that tent are a number of U.S. cities working through the U.S.–Cuba Sister City Association. The European Union supports "town twinning" that in 2003 allocated 12 million euros to some thirteen hundred projects within Europe.

In just 20 years, as of July 1, 2009, Mayors for Peace—organized by the mayors of Hiroshima and Nagasaki—had grown to 2,963 cities in 134 countries and regions. Its 2020 Vision Campaign aims for the complete elimination of nuclear weapons by the year 2020. A major first step will be presentation of the Nuclear Weapons Convention (NWC) to the UN's 65th General Assembly in September 2010. A companion program aims for enhanced rules of war to uphold the inviolability of cities in warfare. As of mid-2008 Mayors for Peace had obtained signatures of the NWC of 82 European Parliament members from 19 European Union states (NWC 2008, 416, 419).

At its seventy-sixth annual meeting in Miami, Florida, in June 2008, the U.S. Conference of Mayors—comprised of cities with populations in excess of thirty thousand—adopted a resolution encouraging its members to participate in the Mayors for Peace nonproliferation efforts and to adopt the Hiroshima-Nagasaki Protocol in support of the UN Decade for Disarmament, 2010–2020 (NWC 2008, 112).

The National League of Cities (NLC) links some 18,000 communities. At the NLC's annual Congressional City Conference, elected officials from around the country visit Washington and lobby their senators and representatives on issues important to their populations. The NLC has proved willing to take positions on controversial subjects: in 2003, it adopted a resolution rejecting certain provisions of the PATRIOT Act because those provisions threaten fundamental rights and civil liberties (NLC 2003).

Mayor Bloomberg of New York tapped into the power of municipal organization on another occasion when, in April 2006, he hosted fifteen big-city mayors at Gracie Mansion to make common cause on handgun control. City government sentiments have been made clear as well as the result of 94 percent of police chiefs nationwide already having formed a handgun-control advocacy group. Within a year, two hundred mayors from forty-six states had signed on to the campaign (Herbert 2007).

In citing so many city and state initiatives, I do not want to deflect attention from my thesis that to forestall disaster necessitates vastly greater citizen engagement. Based on fourteen years as an elected municipal official, I can vouch that invention and progress depend as much or more on citizen initiative as on having a competent mayor, governor, or president. Today's imperative requires cross-border alliances and cross-border democracy.

With so many municipal officials communicating with one another and coordinating efforts on behalf of their citizens, initiating a security conference should not be difficult. The new departure would be to institute direct elections to an international body followed by experiments with cross-border constituency districts as described in Chapter 14. The goal is by no means radical considering that 188 nations have since 1970 been committed, through Article VI of the Non-Proliferation Treaty, "to pursue negotiations in good faith on effective measures relating to cessation of the nuclear arms race at an early date and to nuclear disarmament, and on a treaty on general and complete disarmament under strict and effective international control."

An easy first step for citizens who want to start discussing security would be to learn which of their city or town's elected officials already takes an active part in the National League of Cities, Mayors for Peace, the League of Historical Cities, or a foreign sister city relationship. Ask that person to call a public meeting on the subject of cross-border democracy and security. If citizens fail to find or recruit a helpful elected official, they should field one of their own to run for the local legislative body.

In 1981 I was a Cambridge, Massachusetts, city councilor. The Reagan administration had decided to warn the Soviet Union that the United States was not afraid of nuclear war. The Federal Emergency Management Agency (FEMA) announced a nuclear attack relocation plan, pursuant to which presumed target cities were matched with assumed safe havens. The target populations were instructed to evacuate on alarm to the safe havens.

FEMA had published its plan in regional tabloid newspapers, a copy of which was on each city councilor's desk when we arrived for a Monday night session. In the event of nuclear alert, the plan said, one hundred thousand Cambridge residents were to grab the deeds to their houses, leave behind family pets and firearms, and drive one hundred miles west to Greenfield, Massachusetts, population eighteen thousand.

As an arms-control advocate, I thought, "Now we have them!" If Washington wanted Cambridge's help in planning a war, every Cambridge citizen would learn about it. I moved to hold a public hearing and invite experts to tell us what nuclear war would mean for Cambridge. The nine councilors were a fractious lot, but no one objected. George Kistiakowsky spoke; he had invented the triggering charges that focused the atom bomb's implosion and then served as a science advisor to President Eisenhower. His wife Elaine was one of my precinct leaders. Helen Caldicott lived close by; Everett Mendelsohn taught the history of science at Harvard. These and other highly credentialed witnesses gave testimony about nuclear destruction that no one could dispute. After the lengthy and moving hearing (unforgettable were Helen's final, whispered words, ". . . never again to smell a rose"), I moved that the city prepare and mail a summary of the testimony to all thirty thousand Cambridge households.

Cambridge and Nuclear Weapons: Is There a Place to Hide? told readers how many would be dead and how many would be left to envy the dead at various distances from ground zero at city hall. It reported which nations maintained nuclear arsenals, and it ended with the sentence "Do not assume that someone else can be smarter than you are about this."

To everyone's surprise, the impact was national. Wire services and the *International Herald Tribune* reported on the story, and National Public Radio's "All Things Considered" interviewed me on a national hookup. Charles A. Kimball reported,

> Responsible, honest, and courageous are words seldom used to describe the behavior of government officials these days. Yet such language would not be inappropriate to describe a recent action by the city council of Cambridge, Massachusetts—publication last week of a ten-page booklet entitled *Cambridge and Nuclear Weapons*. Its central message is that the best civil defense is a political offense.
>
> The Cambridge City Council has dared to think about the unthinkable. These nine people decided that uninformed or wishful thinking simply would not do. They faced squarely the

most ominous and frightening issue of our day. And they have dealt with it in a responsible and honest manner.

The Cambridge City Council has set an example for other cities, and more important it has reminded us that in a democracy we are the government. It is our responsibility to decide what we believe is best for ourselves, our families, and our country, and to so inform those who represent us. (*Los Angeles Times*, September 20, 1981)

Requests for copies poured in. As the booklet went to a second and then a third printing, dozens of cities and towns in the United States, Canada, and the British Isles—including New York City, Baltimore, Philadelphia, San Francisco, Toronto, and Vancouver—prepared similar booklets or adopted resolutions opposing municipal war planning, recognizing that the evacuation proposals amounted either to planning for a nuclear war on the assumption that such a war is winnable, or constituted a bluffing game with the Soviet Union. Either way, they substituted for persisting in not offering the world steps to prevent war. FEMA quietly shelved the evacuation plans.

Judging by a joke that found its way to the United States, the Soviet Union's efforts to marshal its own cities to play nuclear chicken met with similar derision. Igor and Ivan meet on the street.

"Ivan, have you heard? The government has announced the nuclear evacuation plans!"

"About time! What are we supposed to do?"

"They want us to take off our clothes, wrap ourselves in a sheet, and crawl slowly to the nearest graveyard."

After a pause, Ivan says, "I understand the graveyard and maybe the sheet, but why crawl?"

"They don't want to cause a panic."

Mayors to the defense of cities!

Cities, the heart of modern civilization and home to half of humanity, are under threat:
—Cities are not safe in a world where there are weapons of mass destruction.
—Cities are not safe in a world in which the rules of war are inadequate and disrespected.

Mayors for Peace demands that the nuclear-armed states of the world each publicly acknowledge that it would be a war crime of the highest order to attack a city with a nuclear weapon or to expose populated areas to radioactive fallout, and to rule out immediately such actions by its armed forces under any circumstances. To be doubly sure that a Hiroshima or a Nagasaki never occurs:
—nuclear weapons must be banned;
—cities must be protected from the scourge of war.

—2020 Vision Campaign

CHAPTER 8

Multilevel Governance: Implications for Democracy and Security

National governments are currently the losers in history's endless power flux. Global corporations, brandishing wealth and influence across political boundaries, operating beyond the regulation of both national laws and international institutions like the European Union and the World Trade Organization, are winners. So are terrorists, armed or soon to be armed with weapons that project power on a scale formerly reserved for entire armies. Nations all too readily sacrifice democracy in the effort to retain security. Individual citizens, facing breaches in their nation-state bulwarks, must scramble to reconfigure both their security arrangements and control over the forces they rely on. Displacement of (somewhat) democratically accountable national power produces a net diminishment of democratic control unless democracy can find new power centers to command.

Opportunities and Pitfalls of Federalism

Let us consider what some of the innovative scholars are saying.
James N. Rosenau observes:

> Viewed in the context of proliferating centers of authority, the
> global stage is thus dense with actors, large and small, for-
> mal and informal, economic and social, political and cultural,
> national and transnational, international and subnational,
> aggressive and peaceful, liberal and authoritarian, who collec-
> tively form a highly complex system of governance on a global
> scale. (Rosenau 2004, 32)

B. Guy Peters and Jon Pierre, in "Multi-Level Governance
and Democracy: A Faustian Bargain?" warn that shrinking
accountability is inherent when convenient multilevel "governance" by appointed authorities, commissions, and agencies
encroaches on the power of hierarchical and elected executives
and legislatures:

> Hierarchy has to a significant extent been replaced by a divi-
> sion of labor, competence, and jurisdiction among largely
> self-regulatory governance processes at different tiers of gov-
> ernment. (Peters and Pierre 2004, 79)

> Multi-level governance could be said to be a way of capital-
> izing on the growing professionalism of regional and local
> authorities. Their increasing assertiveness vis-à-vis central
> government in many jurisdictions is proof of a self-reliance
> that stems in part from having the administrative and organi-
> zational capabilities to make autonomous decisions regarding
> their resource mobilization strategies without having to sub-
> mit to the central state. . . .
>
> Subnational authorities launching ambitious international
> initiatives, even up to the point of signing agreements with

overseas authorities, do so in violation with the constitutional definition of their competencies. (Peters and Pierre 2004, 80)

Helping to propel the multilevel governance explosion, Rosenau notes, is

the ever-greater interdependence and complexity that new electronic and transportation technologies have induced. . . . [T]he rapid shrinking of time and distance. . . has been called a relationship revolution. Today people are so fully and frequently in contact with like-minded others and their interests so fully and frequently overlap, as to engage in organization building and networking processes that call for at least a modicum of governance. The relationship revolution is founded on an organizational explosion that is staggering in its scope. In all parts of the world and at every level of community, people, ordinary folk as well as elites and activists, are coming together to concert their efforts on behalf of shared needs and goals. (Rosenau 2004, 35)

With the death of time and distance, subnational organizations and governments that once operated within the confines of national boundaries are now so inextricably connected to far-off parts of the world that the legal and geographic jurisdictions in which they are located matter less and less. *What matters, instead, are the spheres of authority to which their members are responsive* [emphasis mine]. (Rosenau 2004, 39)

In their essay in *Multi-Level Governance*, Stephen Welch and Caroline Kennedy-Pipe conclude that, following 9/11 and U.S. adoption of the doctrine of preemption, the War on Terror, like the War on Drugs, tends to cripple democracy, in part because "[i]n democracies. . . it is uncommon for international affairs to be electorally significant" (Welch and Kennedy-Pipe 2004, 143). For example,

> the UN Security Council is in the process of being superseded in the role of interpreting and effecting its own resolutions by an American administration bound on pre-emption of the threat supposedly presented by Iraq. Needless to say, similar questions about the role of powerful states can be raised about the operations of the WTO, the International Monetary Fund (IMF), and the WB [World Bank]. (Welch and Kennedy-Pipe 2004, 142)

Ian Bache and Matthew Flinders, in the concluding essay of *Multi-Level Governance*, write:

> While multi-level governance in its different forms may add to the legitimacy of public policy-making through increased efficiency, it may reduce legitimacy in the form of democratic accountability unless new means are found to connect citizens more effectively with the shifting locations of power. . . . Our view is that the evolving structures of multi-level governance are likely to necessitate new forms and models of accountability that seek to build new and innovative conduits between the public and the institutions involved in complex networks. In essence, this may involve a fundamental reappraisal of the meaning of democracy and the role of representative institutions with nation states. . . . We would not expect a "one size fits all" solution to this challenge: it is likely that in the context of different types of multilevel governance, different types of democratic arrangements will be needed to ensure popular consent. (Bache and Flinders 2004, 205)

Exactly. If the nation-state sphere of authority cannot build a democratic means to curtail WMD and prevent war, threatened populations must devise an alternative sphere. Cities and towns are the only political arm within the effective disposal of the threatened populations. If interest-group networking across national boundaries performs global tasks effectively and serves every common concern except security, then populations should place their cities and towns in the game. Not only can municipal networking empower efforts to create world order under enforced law, but the democratic foundation of municipalities can compensate for the drawbacks of the "Faustian bargain" noted by Peters and Pierre.

For any who doubt that wrenching shifts are ahead in how power is layered, consider a 2007 *New York Times* column by University of Maryland professor Gar Alperovitz. British prime minister Tony Blair and California governor Arnold Schwarzenegger, he notes, signed an accord on global warming between the state of California and Great Britain. He quotes Schwarzenegger, "We have the economic strength, we have the population and the technological force of a nation-state. . . . We are a good and global commonwealth. . . . We are the modern equivalent of the ancient city-states of Athens and Sparta" (Alperovitz 2007).

Alperovitz believes Schwarzenegger has "put his finger on a little-discussed flaw in America's constitutional formula. The United States is almost certainly too big to be a meaningful democracy" (Alperovitz 2007). Citing other nations in which power is devolving to regional authorities and the fact that half of the world's two hundred nations created since 1946 were formed as breakaways, Alperovitz thinks that breakup or radical decentralization of power is ahead for the this country.

It is interesting that Schwarzenegger compares California's role with that of Athens and Sparta. One does reflect, though, on how the Greek city-states succumbed to war and were succeeded in leadership by Rome in the West and the Muslims in the East. Our first concern should be (as Alperovitz's is) for democracy, as the highest goal for preservation, the instrument of civic redemption, and civilization's savior. Democracy must be achieved and preserved in the community before one can aspire for it to be effective in a state or nation.

In the United States, much that the public hears about government and democracy in Europe pertains to the European Union. It would be helpful to hear as well about the strengthened municipal democracy that cross-border municipal cooperation has produced. In 1953 one thousand elected representatives from across Europe, meeting at Versailles, adopted the European Charter of Municipal Liberties. The charter addressed a hundred thousand European local governments. The preamble read, "Europe's municipalities, united across frontiers within the Council of European Municipalities, are determined to build, in the interests of their citizens, a free and peaceful Europe." The definition of municipal liberties contained in the charter included this: "Municipalities and their associations have the right to belong to international organizations in order to promote the defense of their interests and their rights, in accordance with the fundamental principles of this Charter."

In 1985 the member states of the Council of Europe agreed on the European Charter of Local Self-Government. At the twentieth anniversary conference in 2005, mayor of The Hague Wim Deetman made it clear that he did not limit his security concerns to crime: "Although local leaders cannot—strictly speaking—guarantee the safety of their citizens, they have a special responsibility: they decide when the level of safety has become unacceptable and then take active measures, by force if needed" (Council of Europe 2006).

Professor Hans Köchler of the University of Innsbruck notes the need to address the fact that citizens currently have but a "rudimentary form of the transnational European concept of citizenship" (Köchler 2000, 152). Under the EU constitution, a citizen can vote to elect members of the European

Parliament and enjoys the right to participate in municipal elections in the place of his or her residence even if not
a national. Köchler calls for the "gradual building of a 'pan-
European public space' consisting of political organizations,
citizens' movements, etc., with a universal European outlook
(to complement the political articulation of the citizens' will
on the level of the nation-state)" (Köchler 2000, 159). In Spain,
municipal corruption prompted non-Spanish residents of
Spain to participate in local politics as both voters and candidates for office. In 2007, 318,517 non-Spanish voters were registered in Spain, according to the *Financial Times* (Crawford
2007). A number of other European countries allow foreigners
to vote locally, generally based on the length of residence in
the host country (Council of Europe 2000).

Creative federalism stimulates the interplay of legislative
initiatives, taxing power, and judicial oversight. At a lower level
of government, imaginative officeholders can initiate reforms
and programs that prevailing opinion would not countenance
for the entire country at once. Initiatives that prevailing opinion
considers overdue can start despite isolated or regional resistance. Innovation emerges piecemeal from a mix of new laws
and the reinterpretation of old laws and constitutions. Political
readiness matures through cycles that respond to crisis, to leadership, or even to spreading good sense.

Benjamin R. Barber says that federalism provides Americans with "two faces":

> [Federalism] is the American argument about nationalism
> and sectionalism, about order and liberty, about sovereignty
> and factionalism, and about wisdom and democracy. It is the
> protean vessel into which Americans have poured their com-
> peting ideologies and their diverse theories of power and lib-
> erty from the time of the founding to the present day. (Barber
> 1998, 134)

Barber quotes two hallowed figures who might serve as expert witnesses for the thesis that today's security crisis compels asking what further usefulness federalism offers. First, Thomas Jefferson:

> Making every citizen an acting member of the government, and in the offices nearest and most interesting to him, will attach him by his strongest feelings to the independence of his country, and its republican constitution. (Barber 1998, 138)

Then, Alexis de Tocqueville:

> A central administration is fit only to enervate the nations in which it exists, by incessantly diminishing their local spirit. Although such an administration can bring together at a given moment, on a given point, all the disposable resources of a people, it injures the renewal of those resources. It may ensure a victory in the hour of strife, but it gradually relaxes the sinews of strength. It may help admirably the transient greatness of a man, but not the durable prosperity of a nation. (Barber 1998, 172)

The Global Perspective: Federalism Writ Large

The universe for which we must devise security has to be grasped in multiple dimensions. To imagine security through force of arms disregards history's lessons about arms races and terrorism's nondeterrable nature. To imagine security as a precipitate of the existence of more democracies forgets how often democracies answer to self-interested power components rather than elections.

To imagine that competing nations, responsive first to the self-interested power centers that run them, can evolve while prevalent current practices prevail into a mutually compatible, strife-free "family of nations," to use an old cliché, disregards the necessity for law enforced on all nations. To imagine supranational enforced law without a supranational mode of democracy to control it disregards the danger of global tyranny, the justified fear of which raises insuperable political opposition to submitting to law that might curtail war. To imagine that supranational democracy and enforced law can be drawn up and "adopted" like the U.S. Constitution disregards the immensity of a task that will require decades of experiment and staged development.

To stave off disaster, people are needed who will reflect simultaneously on nuclear destruction, terrorism, nations, law, law enforcement, democracy, and international institutions. No sense can be made of one part alone. Sixty-five years of dedicating American power, wealth, and enthusiasm to staying ahead in an imperfectly controlled nuclear weapons race have brought the United States to its greatest peril. Sixty-five years of tolerating the fiction that an international institution like the UN, composed of and answerable only to nations, might ever regulate nations' worst propensities have brought all peoples and their civilizations to their greatest peril.

R. B. J. Walker observes that one can appeal to universal truths within states but not between them. In the United States we talk democracy, but when it comes to intercourse with other nations, we address only national interest. Walker concludes, "This double standard comes to define the limits of political possibility" (Walker 1993, 198). He also writes that

> [i]t is not the continuing presence or imminent absence of the state that is in question. It is the meaning of political community (and thus all those questions about "who we are" that have been presumed to have their answer in the principle of state sovereignty) that is radically problematic. (Walker 1993, 209)

> The great ideals of Enlightenment that have informed the dominant doctrines of recent history depend upon its aspirations for universality. But these aspirations have found their most

persuasive expression in the ambitions of particular communities. To seek power, to ask what is to be done, is to covet the
state. (Walker 1993, 194)

The result, when it comes to world order, is that the only model
our thought modes permit is the state writ large, or world government. To which Walker responds:

> [This] vision of historical transformation must be futile. There-
> fore, political "realism" demands only a vigilant, if tragic,
> accommodation with statist fragmentation, and not the stimu-
> lation of utopian hopes for a universalizing global community.
> (Walker 1993, 199)

> To claim that the only alternative to state sovereignty is some
> kind of supranational authority is to engage in the fallacy of
> the domestic analogy. (Walker 1993, 204–205)

Richard Falk catches the essential connection in the age of
globalization between international law and democratization
(Falk 1995). Market forces, religious fundamentalism, and military culture undermine law when they generate war, unrest, and
destabilizing inequities. The treaties that diplomacy achieves,
and the rules that emerge from cases before the International
Court of Justice at The Hague and other international tribunals,
cannot cope with the explosion of supranational commerce and
interdependent economies, employment, and capital flow. The
unresolved conflicts are left to fester and ultimately surrender
to the age-old final arbiter, war, fought with implausible weapons. If rules and rule enforcement cannot discover the spawning
ground of global democracy, disaster is certain.

The Cold War winners forestalled the needed political invention by promoting a version of democracy preoccupied with
economic policy and committed to promoting purist market

approaches to development, with emphasis on privatization, free trade, and deregulation (with exceptions and contradictions abounding, Falk notes, like subsidies, trade protections, and welfare capitalism for the defense industry) (Falk 1995, 110). The world does not need, says Falk, a "cult of democratization spread by financiers, media moguls, and warriors" (Falk 1995, 112). The heart of authentic democracy is rather "unconditional respect for human rights and for the rule of law, including especially respect for international law in relation to uses of military force" (Falk 1995, 111).

To renounce violence is the hardest step, especially for Americans, who fancy their democracy pure and intentions benign yet have enmeshed themselves in an empire that they are told must be patrolled with unprecedented and resentment-provoking force for the sake of pride, patriotism, and prosperity.

On top of failing to renounce violence during its struggle to block socialist-oriented governments, Falk asserts, the United States conflated democracy and capitalism as "part of the end-game being played with socialism" (Falk 1995, 116). To repair the damage done by militarism and consumerism in the name of democracy, "supervening constraints on the political behavior of governments" are needed. "Such constraints require making international law effective *within* states, *giving every citizen the right to a lawful foreign policy as a part of humane governance at the state level* [emphasis mine]" (Falk 1995, 118).

Understanding that everything depends on initiatives by self-selected individuals, Falk would authorize citizens to obtain court orders to force governments to comply with World Court decisions, or at least to obtain advisory opinions about international law (Falk 1995, 123). Economic and political elites—that is, the controlling powers of states—will not "protect the general human interest. . . . Only a transnational social movement animated by a vision of humane governance can offer any hope of extending the domain of democracy" (Falk 1995, 120).

Falk contrasts the effects of globalization from above with those that would follow globalization from below. In the former case, increasingly autocratic political forces and coercive market forces deprive even democratized state/society relations of control. In the latter case, state and market forces are balanced by "agencies of civil society," which are "survival oriented" (Falk 1995, 124–26). Falk would work toward democratizing geopolitical forces "to make citizens more inclined to demand respect for international law as a basis for paying taxes and supporting government" (Falk 1995, 123). In addition to conferring jurisdiction on officials and citizens to challenge in the courts foreign policy that violates international law, Falk recommends giving transnational citizen associations the power to pose questions of international law in the World Court, and creating a second United Nations Assembly.

Falk calls democracy the "indispensable organizing principle," requiring "positive citizenship" that will meet the "greatest challenge," which is "to reconcile the territorial dimensions of citizenship with the temporal dimensions: acting in the present for the sake of the future" (Falk 1995, 253). However, he distinguishes authentic democracy from authoritarian democracy and market democracy, which mislead us from the commitment to human rights and nonviolence that must undergird international law. He warns against a militarist culture that produces peak popularity for leaders when they resort to war, as well as a "fundamentalist cultural mood" that "validates democratically the removal of rights" (Falk 1995, 117).

Falk is right to insist that any democracy relied upon to achieve reasonable goals must be authentic. Authenticity is a function of politics, but the problem is, we distrust politics. Too many were ready to sign on for George W. Bush's Iraq War on the grounds that democracy could be brought to the Middle East with an army.

Neocon apostate Francis Fukuyama exemplifies this distrust of, and consequent disinterest in, politics. He dismisses both neoconservative and "realist" approaches to foreign policy, advancing as the basis for foreign policy legitimacy only the possibility of more nations becoming democratic. He advocates as well a global Community of Democracies that, he thinks, would provide an additional institutional foundation for peace. Fukuyama asserts that a collective of democracies could endow international rules with legitimacy (Fukuyama 2006, 176). John McCain made this proposal a plank of his 2008 presidential campaign's foreign policy platform.

Fukuyama fails, on the other hand, to suggest how more nations might become democratic, how they would mediate their differences, and how to prevent polarization between democracies and nondemocracies. To say as he does that institutions created by the joint actions of separate, sovereign democratic nations will necessarily be legitimate is an unwarranted leap, disproved by his own criticism of the joint policies of the democratic United States and the democratic Great Britain in the Iraq War.

Fukuyama sees that neocon hegemony policy invites the resentment of every other nation and people, progressively eroding the advantages of superior strength. He sees that "realist" reliance on endless manipulating among sovereign powers constitutes no progress over the posture of all against all that resulted in two world wars. His imagination falters, though, when it comes to supranational democracy: "It is doubtful whether we will ever be able to create truly democratic global institutions, particularly if they aspire, like the United Nations, to be globally representative" (Fukuyama 2006, 192).

If authoritarian nations were excluded because they are not democratic, their populations would be excluded as well. But the populations of democracies are represented in global policymaking only indirectly, through representatives appointed by governments that they elect. They have no more direct say about the wisdom and morality of their cities being left to Armageddon than populations of authoritarian governments. Fukuyama implies that to enlarge democracy beyond national borders would never work, on the grounds that the European Union's democratic elements have "run into massive obstacles with regard to both legitimacy and effectiveness" (Fukuyama 2006, 192).

At the same time, Fukuyama says that "[t]he world today does not have enough international institutions that can confer legitimacy on collective action, and creating new institutions that will better balance the requirements of legitimacy and effectiveness will be the prime task for the coming generation (Fukuyama 2006, 155). Such legitimacy he calls horizontal accountability, in contrast with successful rule-making within the "vertical silos we call states" (Fukuyama 2006, 156). One asks, why cannot global democracy become another example of the means by which he says that "societies are increasingly interpenetrated economically and culturally" (Fukuyama 2006, 156).

Fukuyama identifies four contemporary approaches to foreign policy and brands each of them faulty: hegemony, realist power politics between sovereignties, isolationist nationalism, and law-based comity. About the last, he observes, "there are liberal internationalists who hope to transcend power politics altogether and move to an international order based on law and institutions" (Fukuyama 2006, 7). Perhaps Fukuyama's use of *liberal* in this context constitutes the habitual Republican opprobrium assigned to those who disagree with them. His use of *power* to modify *politics* implies that power—in the military and economic sense in which he means it—is separable from politics, but all politics is power politics. That is the purpose of politics, to allocate power, which precisely explains why politics belongs in the global arena. Politics is the only way in which people can counterbalance the power of wealth, media access, leadership charisma, and, above all in foreign affairs, military power.

Reliance on enforced international law is indeed intended to transcend reliance on the military. What "liberal internationalists," if that is what they are, and Fukuyama alike miss is that law rests on politics, and until we achieve a global polis (not world government), we will not achieve legal comity.

In his chapter "Social Engineering and Development," Fukuyama provides an interesting summary of efforts to promote democracy. He concludes that successful democracy promotion has exhibited one of three characteristics. The first example describes initiatives from within the society; the second depicts the semiauthoritarian regimes that operate under some internal compulsion; the third involves countries in which the population has aspired to changes like joining the European Union. He finally gets around to saying that public participation and democracy are essential to good governance (Fukuyama 2006, 137–41), but he never makes a people-to-people connection. He goes on to criticize the organizational shortcomings of the American "soft power" that might help promote democracy around the world. Too many agencies, he argues; too little coordination and funding.

David Held thinks that democratic accountability will have to be imposed on many nongovernmental as well as governmental agencies, such as corporations and media owners. He advocates pragmatic recognition that democratic accountability will have to be introduced by the

> multiple lodging of the rights and obligations of democratic law in the organizational charters of the agencies and associations which make up the spheres of politics, economics, and civil society. . . . A cosmopolitan democracy must always be an ensemble of organizations, associations, and agencies pursuing their own projects, whether these be economic, social, or

cultural; but these projects must always also be subject to the
constraints of democratic processes and a common structure
of political action" (Held 1995, 277–78).

Held counts municipalities as one form of "democratic associations" that can lead to the "recovery of an intensive and participatory democracy at local levels as a complement to the
public assemblies of the wider global order" (Held 1995, 234).

Mary Kaldor elaborates on the idea that a "horizontal political culture" might generate an accountable means of imposing
order on the world. "There have to be formal rules for accountability—say, direct elections to an international parliament or
an assembly of local territorial units" (Kaldor 1995, 89). The
units can be "national, regional, or municipal" (Kaldor 1995, 90).
Kaldor contrasts the usefulness of such a development with an
alternative model, in which "advanced industrial countries form
a coalition based around a military alliance or set of military
treaties" (Kaldor 1995, 85). In the latter case, she predicts—and
it seems to have come to pass—ethnicity or cultural nationalism
would pit one group, like the Western European nations, against
the "'other'—the 'other' being non-European (orthodox, Muslim,
black) and characterized by fundamentalism, chaos, violence,
nationalism" (Kaldor 1995, 87).

In *Cosmopolitan Democracy*, Daniele Archibugi (1995)
asks, "Is it possible to limit the state's monopoly of decision-
making at the international level without ending with a world
state?" (Archibugi 1995, 133). The challenge, he says, is "to
give voice to citizens in the world community in an institutional mode parallel to states" (Archibugi 1995, 135). Archibugi
notes that Article 22 of the UN Charter states that "The General
Assembly may establish such subsidiary organs as it deems necessary for the performance of its functions" (Archibugi 1995,
142). Nothing prevents the establishment of a consultative Second Assembly elected directly by citizens. An alternative device,

Archibugi suggests, would be to provide for citizen election of one of the five national representatives that each member nation sends to the General Assembly.

Internationalism as a Political Assignment

Aside from a few authors like these, the prospect of democratic international governance gets discredited on the ground that the world is bewilderingly big, cultures are too diverse for agreement about values and priorities ever to emerge, and too few societies are composed of citizens on a civic par with those of so-called advanced countries, whether due to a lag in historical progress in education and economic development, or due to innate inferiority. (The last of these exemplifies the not-infrequent necessity of giving up on persuasion and summoning every resource to outpower and defeat the opponent.)

What is it that doubters about internationalism think people from diverse cultures cannot agree on? That cities ought not be incinerated? That ecological balance is requisite to species survival? That there ought to be basic human rights? The very ones who underestimate the self-governing capacity of certain foreigners are the ones who think so little of the average American's capacity that they substitute opinion manipulation for honest debate in domestic politics. After all, if you subscribe to the democratic postulates that government belongs to the public, and that average people can vote knowledgeably and objectively, no logical impediment remains, other than surmounting communication barriers, to regional and international institutions for law enforcement.

It would help to admit the extent to which nations are employed for the private ends of the groups that control their governments. If Americans truly could believe, to the point of acting on the belief, that government should concern itself primarily with the public's interest (and security would surely top the list of those interests), and if they believed that free enterprise and free markets meant keeping the government out of commercial matters, then to enlarge democracy to supranational matters would follow.

Despite the absence of intention to affront or harm any individual, the global economic system poisons the wells of cultural tradition and jerry-builds a profit-motivated "security" system for sale in deadly segments. Anyone who doubts that security as national leaders define it harbors fatal contradictions need only compare the purported absence of intention of harming noncombatants with the hundreds of thousands of slaughtered civilians in the "preventive" wars of our age, and with the infinite carnage that the tolerance of nuclear proliferation presages.

So let Washington, Damascus, and Teheran comply as they will with the dictates of money, strategy, religion, and nationalist pride. Let them perpetuate the myth that their war preparations are aimed at armies. Let us respond to war's inevitable engulfment both of populations and civilization, and to terrorism's self-glorification through war under another name. Let us seek order under democratically accountable enforced law where the power to seek it is available (at least initially): in cities and towns. Let us champion self-defense by the targets of the missiles and bombs, who, after all, are us.

No need to shortchange national allegiances or even to overcome the very human tendency to see Stalin or Hitler reborn in the leaders of our national rivals. But let us renounce group victimization and acknowledge that the targeting of urban centers constitutes universal victimization. Let us not hear that we are targeted as Americans or Christians or Jews, even when some of the most dangerous men alive say it. Let us understand the generic human peril and reach out, through the political bodies within our reach, to all the targets around the world.

The boundaries that must be enforced today are not land boundaries but weapons boundaries. Intercontinental ballistic missiles made land boundaries a mockery fifty years ago;

terrorists have made them a nullity. The increasingly global nature of weapons creation defeats whatever inclination national governments might have to restrain violence. Because global production power, marketing, and resource exploitation have become interdependent, arms-control politics must surround the economic and ideological sources and uses of power. Democracy must usurp monetary power as it usurped the king's power. Because monetary power is global, democracy must be global. Because democracy is never a gift, it must be built where the power to build is available.

Great Britain's North American colonies in 1776 were more like countries than states within a common sovereignty. Their immense geographical spread, the primitive means of travel and communication, and the diversity of history and culture all weighed against the colonies being united. Some of the smartest men around said so, but as it happened they did not sense the unity that had developed or accurately gauge the availability of mature, courageous, and creative political thinkers and organizers.

Having come so far in 233 years and disproved woeful predictions of some of the most brilliant of our founders' generation, why do we lack the optimistic imaginings needed to export our political success? "Be like us" is our exhortation, rather than "Join us." R. B. J. Walker surmises that the modern mind, for whom the ideals of the Enlightenment have expired, is disabled when challenged to "aspire to universality." Domestically, we live in multiple societies: the economic society that organizes the components of sustenance, shelter, and financial stability; the social societies that provide emotional and recreational support; the religious societies for those who want otherworldly assurances; and the political societies of nation, state, and city to allocate civic power. The societies overlap and interleave. The fatal omission, in the nuclear age, is a security society.

I have wondered what life was like in a time and place as insecure as ours has become but where the insecurity was acknowledged because it was more comprehensible. Imagine the North American frontier when Indians killed, for instance, Abraham Lincoln's grandfather, and Lyndon Johnson's grandmother survived a Comanche raid in a root cellar under her East Texas cabin (Caro 1982, 21). Or the island of Milos when the Athenians told the citizens, before slaughtering the men and enslaving their wives and children, "[T]he strong do what they can and the weak suffer what they must" (Thucydides, 352). Or Baku in the tenth century when, exposed to Corsair pillage, citizens built the round tower that you can visit today, to which the entire population retreated when sails rose on the horizon. Or consider the story within the story of *Don Quixote*, fictionalizing Miguel Cervantes's actual experience after Algerian pirates sold him into slavery.

How would one characterize the difference between the security choices of the past and today's choices? Formerly, the choices have ranged from moving to East Texas and locating the root cellar under the cabin, to building that tower by the Caspian Sea, to embarking on a voyage in the face of piracy, to declaring independence from a colossal empire. Does making the right choice today between hunkering down and waging preemptive war on the one hand, and adopting world governance of security and universal, enforced law and disarmament on the other require greater foresight, leadership, risk, or confidence?

The world's peoples are not wild dogs of irreconcilable strains, nor are they spurred on by inevitable antagonisms. In the United States, at least, we are not victims of irresistible historic forces although we contribute more than our share to the profit-driven global economy that exploits with no intention of injuring individuals but drives millions from their lands, from their livelihoods, and denies them nutrition. To a greater degree than most of the world, we are a marketing-targeted, consumption-driven, politically passive herd, headed for a cliff.

Think of a nonswimmer in water over his head, thrashing for a handhold, pumping arms for an ounce of buoyancy, screaming for help. He will find help where it can be found and reject the bewilderment that invites disaster. Go down if we must, though we needn't, but let it be holding hands with the rest of humanity as resisting sharers of twenty thousand years of human progress.

[Adlai] Stevenson renewed a proposal. . . that disarmament should be the major theme of the United States. [President] Kennedy remarked that it did not seem to be a popular issue with the public or Congress. He said that he knew how much disarmament meant to the rest of the world, and it was an issue he could use against the Soviet Union: "We are ready for inspection; they aren't. . . ."

Although Stevenson agreed, he told the President: "We can't do this effectively if we ourselves equivocate. Your first decision, Mr. President, must be to make sure that you yourself are genuinely for general and complete disarmament. We must go for that. Everything else in our program derives from it. Only total disarmament will save the world from the horror of nuclear war as well as from the mounting expense of the arms race. Your basic decision must be to identify yourself with a new approach to disarmament. This must be our principal initiative in the United Nations." . . . (Schlesinger 1965, 478)

Kennedy. . . saw little opportunity for progress on the issue and, as a result, viewed it as a measure of political warfare. Kennedy remarked that he understood the "propaganda" importance of pushing the issue.

—from *The Papers of Adlai E, Stevenson, vol. 8: Ambassador to the United Nations, 1961–1965.*

PART III

IMPEDIMENTS

One impediment to security, largely unrecognized or unacknowledged, is an ideology that holds violent confrontation
between nations and peoples as inevitable and even praise-
worthy. Another impediment is the disassembly of democratic
governance's essential elements. Both demonstrate why a subnational nexus of democratic effort on behalf of security is
essential. First, the ideology.

I suppose the most significant of all the decisions of that nature which we made was the one that denied atomic secrets to the Russians. Secretary Stimson, whose judgment I greatly respected, proposed that we share these secrets with the Russians. Stimson was no soft-headed idealist in making this proposal. He stated that if we did not disclose them, the Russians would become suspicious of us, would feverishly work to develop a fission bomb of their own, and the world would be divided by distrust and tension for decades to come. . . .

I was among those who opposed Stimson, along with Jim Forrestal, Tom Clark, and Fred Vinson. . . . But I'm afraid that I drew my conclusion as a practicing politician and that my position, Los Alamos notwithstanding, had little scientific basis. . . .

I often wonder now what different turn our relations with the Russians would have taken had Stimson's argument prevailed over mine. I certainly think we made our decision too casually and, with a quarter century of perspective to apply to the moment, I also think we were wrong in the decision we made. (Anderson 1970, 68–69)

—Senator Clinton P. Anderson of New Mexico (referring to the period when he was President Truman's Secretary of Agriculture)

CHAPTER 9

The Ideology of Eternal Conflict

The Lure and Peril of Hegemony

Samuel P. Huntington is the revered theorist of establishment foreign policy "realists." His prescription for world order in *The Clash of Civilizations and the Remaking of World Order* is simplicity itself. Each of the nine world civilizations, he says, must field a core state that is accepted as the hegemon and arbiter within that civilization, and together the nine core states must enforce global law and order. The one rule they should follow is never to intervene in a dispute between another civilization's core state and that state's dependents, even or perhaps especially when the core state is flouting international law (Huntington 1996, 316). In a dust jacket blurb, Henry Kissinger, the epitome of power brokers, raved back in the twentieth century that the book makes us understand "the realities of global politics in the next century" (Huntington 1996, 226).

Of course! What could be more useful for hegemonic policy than to find that we have a core state responsibility? "Deep imperatives within American culture, however, impel the United States to be at least a nanny if not a bully in international affairs," Huntington writes (Huntington 1996, 226–27). All that is left is to persuade the European Union to accept a back seat; China to be reasonable; South America to agree on its own core state; sub-Saharan Africa to find a possible core state; and the Middle East, North Africa, and Indonesia to choose one among themselves to impose leadership over Islam's widespread civilization.

Quoting Michael Walzer, Huntington says it is true that humans share a few minimal moral "negative injunctions, most likely, rules against murder, deceit, torture, oppression, and tyranny" (Huntington 1996, 318). Huntington does not find Walzer's inventory of prohibited practices to be enough on which to base "universalism," which seems to be his characterization of international law. Western universalism, he concludes, is vacuous.

Huntington lauds a 1989 speech by President Wee Kim Wee of Singapore describing the four values that permit Singapore's diverse ethnic population to find cultural identity, and an ensuing white paper that added a fifth value. Huntington observes that these five values—nation before community, family as basic unit of society, community support for the individual, consensus, and harmony between races and religions—would also find support among Westerners, revealing, he says, a commonality to build on. However, he does not seem to think that Asians would find reciprocal commonality in the values that Westerners would add to the list: rule of law, rights of the individual, freedom of expression, the contest of ideas to find truth, and political participation and competition. These values, presumably, we must guard within our Western borders. One is hardly surprised that, having prescribed a world of competing hegemony, Huntington concludes on his last page that while "law and order is the first prerequisite of civilization," it seems to be evaporating, "yielding to barbarism, generating the image of an unprecedented phenomenon, a global Dark Ages, possibly descending on humanity" (Huntington 1996, 320).

People like Kissinger who devote careers to the war system laud such conclusions. Another of Huntington's admirers, Jimmy Carter's national security advisor Zbigniew Brzezinski, wrote a dust jacket endorsement calling Huntington's work, "an intellectual tour de force: bold, imaginative, and provocative. A seminal work. . . ." Huntington returned the favor a year later in his cover blurb for Brzezinski's *The Grand Chessboard*: "the book we have been waiting for: a clear-eyed, tough-minded definitive exposition of America's strategic interests. . . . [A] masterful synthesis. . . in the grand tradition of Bismarck." Paul Wolfowitz also chimes in on the dust jacket with "Brzezinski has established himself as. . . one of the leading practitioners of the art of strategy."

Brzezinski writes that "America stands at the center of an interlocking universe, one in which power is exercised through consensus, even though that power originates ultimately from a single source, namely, Washington, D.C. And that is where the power game has to be played, and played according to America's domestic rules" (Brzezinski 1997, 21). He admits, and clearly regrets, that "American hegemony involves the exercise of decisive influence but, unlike the empires of the past, not of direct control" (Brzezinski 1997, 35). Eurasia is too big, he says. Our resources must be deployed on the chessboard carefully, selectively, deliberately.

Brzezinski regrets as well that "America is too democratic at home to be autocratic abroad. This limits the use of America's power, especially its capacity for military intimidation" (Brzezinski 1997, 35). His concern is that we not be led to sacrifice sovereignty by either reducing our global engagement or embracing multilateralism (Brzezinski 1997, 36).While our global power should be preserved in the short run, that power should be utilized for "the long-run transformation of it into increasingly institutionalized global cooperation" (Brzezinski 1997, 40). No sooner does he make this constructive-sounding statement, though, than he lapses into what I would call empire-speak: "To put it in a terminology that hearkens back to the more brutal age of ancient empires, the three grand imperatives of imperial geostrategy are to prevent collusion and maintain security dependence among the vassals, to keep tributaries pliant and protected, and to keep the barbarians from coming together" (Brzezinski 1997, 40).

Unlike Huntington, for whom the future depends on endlessly balancing hegemonies of the respective civilizations, Brzezinski seems able to imagine a future in which world order might safely replace American suzerainty. "In the course of the next several decades, a functioning structure of global cooperation, based on geopolitical realities, could thus emerge and gradually assume the mantle of the world's current 'regent,' which has for the time being assumed the burden of responsibility for world stability and peace" (Brzezinski 1997, 215). In the meantime, though, narrow concerns like containing weapons proliferation, eliminating economic injustice, safeguarding the environment, and combating local wars, should yield to the "central realities of global power" (Brzezinski 1997, 214).

Zbigniew Brzezinski, facing the realities of a world too complex for one nation, coalition, or institution to control, and increasingly dangerous for the United States after George W. Bush's hostilities, concludes that reliance must be placed in the American people. In *Second Chance*, he appeals to the next president to improve public education in foreign policy. He says that to be effective, a president's sense of the historical moment must coincide with the gut feelings of the American people (Brzezinski 2007, 179). Yet he bemoans the abysmal foreign affairs ignorance of most Americans and their seduction away from civic responsibilities by affluence and greed. He judges Americans socially unattractive to other peoples because of American devotion to self-gratification and consumer orientation. Despite being the custodians of great power, we are ignorant about the world and lack both civic education and a sense of civic obligation.

Brzezinski knows that time is limited, saying that the administration elected in 2008 will have the "second chance" and that there will be no third chance. He does not, however, imagine a global institutional arrangement other than the traditional one of sovereign nations operating through diplomacy. He does suggest that in engaging that diplomacy the United States should be willing to compromise, honor the world's diversities, and compromise some aspects of sovereignty (Brzezinski 2007, 215). Yet, he barely mentions the United Nations and judges that the European Union will never express a common will.

Brzezinski's conclusions, though not his recommendations, cry for a better medium through which societies might communicate than national governments. He recognizes and regrets that big media and big money control policy. He sees that lobbying influence on Congress and the White House, perniciously controlling policy, has expanded beyond corporate money to include even that of foreign governments. The missing third force, Brzezinski thinks, is American citizens who are not ignorant of foreign affairs and who do respect human dignity. He does not acknowledge that such citizens actually exist, however, and seeks no medium through which, if they do exist, they might exert influence or communicate with activists abroad.

The late professor Edward Said of Columbia University, in contrast, judged that hegemony perpetuates the Cold War. In his essay about Huntington's book, Said, who was born in Jerusalem of Christian Palestinian parents, observes, "So strong and insistent is Huntington's notion that other civilizations necessarily clash with the West, and so relentlessly aggressive and chauvinistic is his prescription for what the West must do to continue winning, that we are forced to conclude that he is really most interested in continuing and expanding the Cold War. . . . It is as a very brief and rather crudely articulated manual in the art of maintaining a wartime status in the minds of Americans and others that Huntington's essay has to be understood" (Said 2002, 570–71).

Huntington, Said thought, wants to "mobilize nationalist passions" because his aim is to manage conflict, not resolve it:

"Far from being an arbiter between civilizations, Huntington is a partisan, an advocate of one so-called civilization over all others" (Said 2002, 573). Said's hope, on the other hand, addressed the way cultures "enter into partnerships to share one another's music and literatures. This sort of cooperative, collective enterprise is what one misses in the proclaimers of an undying clash between cultures: the lifelong dedication that has existed in all modern societies among scholars, artists, musicians, visionaries, and prophets to try to come to terms with the Other, with that other society or culture that seems so foreign and so distant" (Said 2002, 583).

> The overwhelming evidence [is that] today's world is in fact a world of mixtures, of migrations, of crossings over. . . . In any case, a number of political scientists, economists, and cultural analysts have for some years been speaking of an integrative world system, largely economic, it is true, but nonetheless knitted together, overriding many of the clashes spoken of so hastily and imprudently by Huntington. (Said 2002, 587)

Cultural barriers and national pride will bow, Said predicted, to the "benign globalism already to be found, for instance, in the environmental movement, in scientific cooperation, in the universal concern for human rights, in concepts of global thought that stress community and sharing over racial, gender, or class dominance" (Said 2002, 590).

Nation-centered thinking continues to impose its top-down perspective as policy analysts wrestle with the post-9/11 terrorist threat. Philip Bobbitt's discouraging study *Terror and Consent* calls terrorist attacks inevitable, like natural disasters. The best that can be done is manage the risk (Bobbitt 2008, 216). The primary aim of wars against terror must be to preclude the "collapse of effective democratic government" (Bobbitt 2008, 215).

Bobbitt concludes that terrorism must be attacked preemptively, or precursively, as he prefers to say. The trouble is, he winds up sounding like a realist power-balancer. The intervention should not be unilateral, but through an alliance of democracies, the strategy of Fukuyama, McCain, and others, which Bobbitt claims that he invented while serving in the Clinton administration (Bobbitt 2008, 445). Interventions need, as well, the legitimacy of law—"the law that must undergird war," as he puts it (Bobbitt 2008, 215). A legal doctrine must be found that explains why a nation intervenes.

The time for intervention comes when humanitarian concerns and strategic concerns intersect. This test was met in Haiti, Rwanda, Afghanistan, and Bosnia, as it was, Bobbitt says, when the United States entered World War I. He thinks it too soon to tell whether the Iraq invasion qualified (Bobbitt 2008, 245–51). He criticizes Lee Feinstein and Anne Marie Slaughter, who, in "A Duty to Prevent" (Feinstein and Slaughter 2004), favored intervening in North Korea to prevent nuclear arming, but not in China. Law, Bobbitt observes, necessitates consistency (Bobbitt 2008, 471–74).

Bobbitt would use the democratic coalition of the United States, Great Britain, and NATO to establish secure areas of freedom, the rule of law, decent living standards, and free trade, which, as they expand, would shrink the operations of terrorists. Done right, it should be possible to develop international law without "decades-long warfare [that] eventually compelled consensus" (Bobbitt 2008, 475). He continues:

> If we are to wring modification from the legal structure of the society of states without the benefit of the exhaustion and devastation that accompanies epochal wars, then we must look for a different link between WMD, crimes against humanity, and global, networked terrorism than that provided by the legal relationship of states to each other.
>
> That linkage is the states' strategic relationship to terror. It is the awful prospect of unprecedented civilian suffering that can unite the states of the world once the conjunction of

WMD, global terrorism, and humanitarian crises is confronted.
What leader can contemplate the immediate deaths of more
than 200,000? (Bobbitt 2008, 475)

This is correct and a premise of this book, but it will take
serious nudging to get states to change habits cemented with
patriotic fervor, religious faith, ethnic jealousy, and economic
dependence. Bobbitt is good at showing what is new and different about states today, but does not seem to imagine any players but the states, least of all citizens. For him the citizens' role
is passive: to grant consent. Falling back on state action, he
embraces the old bipolar division of democracies and others
and fails to improve our chances. As he concedes, he aims only
to manage the risk. He seems not to imagine universal, progressive disarmament and war prevention, or an enforcement mechanism and the companion suprastate democracy mechanism
needed to make disarmament and war prevention feasible.

Bobbitt comes closest to the thrust of these chapters in
searching for forces that might drive nations to cooperate in law
enforcement. He suggests that NGOs might pressure states to
follow "best state practices" by offering to confer legitimacy in
return for following rules (Bobbitt 2008, 507). Excellent, I say.
NGOs certainly ought to play a role, but they will never be able to
exert enough pressure on states or to invent the people-to-people
couplings that can slip under the bars of authoritarian nation rule
and past the bought-and-sold mores of corporate globalism. Erskine Childers and Brian Urquhart, in their report *Renewing the
United Nations System*, write that "the most thoughtful of leaders in the universe of NGOs are the first to acknowledge that they
cannot provide the central sustaining mechanism that is needed"
(Childers and Urquhart 1994, 174).

As the putative WMD targets, cities can scarcely be denied a
voice, even in nondemocracies. Municipal security conferences
would create that voice. Bobbitt moves in the right direction,

though he fails to identify an agency through which threatened populations might reach one another other than simply "democracy," which excludes the populations of nondemocracies (to the glee, doubtless, of terrorists) and falls short of creating an accountability mechanism that must accompany global law enforcement. Notwithstanding, Bobbitt is on the right track:

> [G]lobal governance for the twenty-first century must be based on the primacy of individuals as members of self-chosen and overlapping groups rather than on the primacy of nations. We must move from state sovereignty based on the role of state citizenship in the global institutions of governance, to a sovereignty based on respect for human rights; from the right of states to develop weapons of their own choosing to the right of societies to be free of predation, including the threat of nuclear annihilation that inevitably accompanies nuclear proliferation; from the rights of states simply to determine the application of their own criminal laws and leave it at that, to the responsibility not to harbor and facilitate the activities of terrorists who target innocent persons abroad. (Bobbitt 2008, 507–508)

The municipal security congress will directly undermine one of the central tenets of terrorists, one that Bobbitt correctly identifies: he says that the state of terror justifies its aim of disrupting consensual choices like elections, free market operations, religious freedom, and human rights (especially the rights of women) "on the grounds that, in a state of consent, there are no innocent civilians. The process of consent implicates every citizen in the decisions taken by governments in their names" (Bobbitt 2008, 206).

Bobbitt's concluding chapter is brilliantly titled: "A Plague Treatise for the Twenty-First Century." He explains that plague treatises were written during the Middle Ages by clueless doctors and clerics to explain to the clueless multitudes what caused plagues. Blame was placed on sin, heresy, racial defects, and so on. "Today," says Bobbitt, "terrorism is not much better understood than plague was then" (Bobbitt 2008, 521).

Bobbitt thinks we must develop new "conceptual tools" comparable to the "intellectual movement" like that which enabled the Cold War "nuclear strategies" (Bobbitt 2008, 522). Surely a better standard for wise statecraft exists than the Cold War's nuclear arms race! What is not new under the sun is the choice between law and lawlessness. Within nations, law is chosen and most citizens live securely. Among states, competition for supremacy in violence remains the choice. Terrorists are ragtag hustlers on the chaotic fringes, who capitalize on state and corporate lawlessness to advance their private pursuits. They resemble the camp followers who used to accompany armies that advanced on foot—profiteering purveyors of food and clothing, prostitutes, gamblers, and cut-throats.

In the nuclear age, to tolerate lawless fringes is suicidal. Law must become universal; nations must submit; and citizens must force the submission and erect a democratic structure with which to supervise the necessary allocations of power. Bobbitt is right that law has to be backed up by force. "Preemption of terrorist attacks, active counterproliferation, and preventive intervention to forestall human rights abuses like genocide or other gross violations of human rights all have roles to play" (Bobbitt 2008, 529). He is wrong, I believe, to think that force not predicated on universal authority can succeed.

Force mustered by democracies, however well intentioned, can never claim to act on behalf of all. Force on behalf of all is the only force that might succeed in steadily, proportionately surrendering the capacity for violence to the nonviolent force of courts and policing. While Bobbitt champions order and insists that the United States limit its actions to legitimate, lawful steps, he does not seem to contemplate a common surrender of reliance on force or, to be precise, the evolution of force from the force of war to the force of law enforcement. Bobbitt sees that torture, punishment of civilians, and the failure to impose control through elections delegitimize defense against terrorism, but seems not to imagine an international arrangement other than the traditional, endless struggle among nations, ameliorated by treaties.

While Bobbitt is a great believer in the law and eloquent concerning the necessity for the United States to adhere, when it comes to enforcement, he thinks the United States must predominate, with the assistance of other democracies, because it possesses "global interests and global power, . . . [its] constitutional arrangements are consistent with the doctrine of transparent sovereignty. . . [and] we do not believe that any other great power would be markedly less arrogant, less self-interested, less obsessed with increasing its power at the expense of its allies" (Bobbitt 2008, 497).

To me, this sounds like a prescription for lawlessness— attempted law enforcement by a self-proclaimed stong man globally interested, but not "markedly" less self-interested. Just the environment in which scalawags thrive.

Circumvent "All Against All"

To resist the nation-driven—or, to be kinder, the nation-tolerated—war system, calls for more than an exchange of ideas. Some million or two or three of us must gain sufficient power to place before targeted populations a model of enforced law from which enough of the people of the world can benefit, to deprive military and economic autocrats, whether American, Chinese, Russian, or Islamic, of the hate-provoking power monopoly that the nations endlessly, bloodily, and futilely have bowed before.

If people want to devote more intelligence to social instead of private benefit, and I believe they do, what should they do? Travel, communication, and war have distended populations across borders, into one another's areas. Publics are contiguous without regard to proximity. With national diplomacy and power-balancing in thrall to the military, municipal governments are one available agency and potential power base by which to lead exposed populations toward collective defense. Cities and towns are the only governments that putative victim populations might hope to control. If the victims will heed survival instincts, a political route can emerge that will force national governments to see that unless all populations are protected, all may die.

National governments have more on their minds than their populations, even though people are quite literally the only thing of value, for whose benefit governments at any level exist. National governments have a variety of masters, some democratic some of the time and some never. Among the masters of all are financial, ideological, and military interests for whom populations serve either as chips in a bluffing game called deterrence, or raw material for wealth, soldiers, and votes. Now terrorists have changed the rules. When terrorists acquire the means to hold entire populations hostage, national sovereignty will lose its reason to exist. There will be global polity or none, and the roots will have to extend deeper than Washington, Beijing, and Moscow.

The founders of the United States assumed that politics and government would prove what I would call everyman's avocation. What an error that, having achieved political liberty and founded a federal system that enables a free society to flourish on a gigantic scale, we neglect to enlarge the sound idea to the dimensions of today's crisis. Instead, we retreat behind the wall of nationalism that events have rendered primitive. The terrorist threat of weapons of mass destruction imposes dangers so prodigious that instinct says avoidance must be cosmic and technologically advanced to boot. One person's effort seems trivial. The result has been civic disengagement.

Can't Say We Weren't Warned

Disengagement in a land where freedom was intended to harness our lives, liberties, and sacred fortunes is hardly a new peril. A university teacher of mine, William J. Newman, addressed it in a book on the "end of history," *Liberalism and the Retreat from Politics*. The tragic result and danger of ending history, Newman said, of losing knowledge about it and respect for its lessons, is to be locked in the present and to forfeit the chance to achieve a future. "The future becomes a process of shrugging one's shoulders." (Newman 1964, 29).

To shape the future, one has to entertain new ideas and solutions. Newman defined a person who does so as a liberal. In contrast, the conservative "lives in the myth of a fixed and happy past. . . . The conservative likes things that are dead because they are safe; he flourishes in an era of the loss of history because change upsets him, and he hopes to avoid it" (Newman 1964, 29). The liberal knows that freedom means the "willingness to experiment through change. He withers in the pessimism that can see no promise but repetition" (Newman 1964, 29). As Newman states, "The political cost of the loss of history is a loss of the idea of politics as the arena in which historical forces are at work to create a future different from the present. . . . Intellectual belief in the possibility of rational, willed, and controlled change collapses" (Newman 1964, 64–65). (Were he alive, Newman would be amused at Francis Fukuyama's judgment in *The End of History* that history has reached a plateau, or "end," given that Fukuyama was chief of policy planning in the State Department of the conservatives' favorite president, Ronald Reagan.)

Liberals who do entertain change have become, Newman believed, so pessimistic they have stopped inventing. They hope at best to "get through events on nerve" (Newman 1964, 32). Newman quotes some of his equally prescient contemporaries. E. H. Carr in *What Is History?* thought the most disturbing result of a "waning of faith in reason among the intellectuals and the political thinkers. . . [is] the loss of the pervading sense of a world in perpetual motion" (Newman 1964, 40). David Riesman's *The Lonely Crowd* said that "[t]he other-directed intrinsically lacks the ability to innovate. . . . Politics ceases to be the means by which man and society transcend themselves. . . . Politics provides no fulcrum for change" (Riesman, Glazer, and Denney 1950, 42). In commentary on C. Wright Mills's *The Power Elite*, Newman reflects "[i]nstead of a society in which no one does anything, there is a small group that supposedly does everything. . . . The question of how to live with it will not be found in the past exactly because the past failed to prevent the giant from becoming Goliath" (Newman 1964, 50). He also suggests that "[t]he past has failed to provide us with solutions and must, therefore, be banished from our thinking today" (Newman 1964, 52).

My goal is to beseech the reader to honor the founders, to heed warnings from the 1960s, and to explore civic invention. A reader who fancies herself liberal is asked to measure up to Newman's compliment, and if conservative, to read with an open mind, especially if there is inclination to disprove Newman's affront.

To acknowledge enough concern to entertain political experiment is the first condition I would ask the reader to accept. The second is time—willingness to take steps toward a system that will need four or five decades to mature while the completed form remains obscure. In other words, experiment patiently. Little gets invented in the short term, while nothing long term that is novel can be expected to share a comfortable resemblance to what one sees today. Richard Falk, in *A Global Approach to National Policy*, observes that "there can be no final solution of the problem of world order, but only a series of transitional solutions" (Falk 1975, 239).

CHAPTER 10

The Disconnect: Nation, Power, Citizens, Democracy, and Law (Civil Order's Five Elements)

Citizenship in the most powerful nation ought to confer power. What Americans think history and wealth promised them, though, dimmed on 9/11 when they witnessed the dress rehearsal for a hellish end at the hands of shadowy fanatics. Little wonder the country is slow to focus. The foolish choice of preemptive war in Iraq at least showed what not to do.

Our civic resources are composite; the parts have to connect. Nation, power, citizens, democracy, and law are the parts. The complacency that civic self-adulation induces blurs the distinctions. We glorify nation, dissipate power, counterfeit democracy, and sidestep law.

Nation

Democratic nationhood seems so fine no law should stand above it. Whatever our nation does deserves a pass because it is a democracy with a glorious history. Whether citizens retain power to control their nation has grown irrelevant because voting is accepted as the apotheosis of power, regardless whether it affects outcomes and despite the shift of power from elected government to the military, to economic centers, to ideology, and now to terrorists, who are destroyers of law, order, and human kindness.

In the United States those in predominant control and the supplicants to them—the protesters and petition signers, and the lobbyists for peace organizations—rely too much on the nation. From the viewpoint of policy formation, a country, any country, belongs to power holders, not power supplicants. So long as the nation was thought the indispensable shield, there seemed little choice but to render it exclusive homage. September 11, though, signaled the limitations of the nation's defender role, a transformation that nuclear-armed terrorists will complete if they destroy cities. As terrorists have ended globally the national monopoly on armed force, corporate globalization has reduced national financial regulation, and travel and communication technology have empowered individuals, both those seeking peace and order, and those bent on destruction.

Nations have become humankind's grandest and most villainous creation. One does not have to love one's country less to recognize that nationalism has become the impediment to security from the nuclear destruction now at the doorstep. Nations are as indispensable as ever. But global problems call for global institutions.

In *The Wrath of Nations*, William Pfaff calls the advent of nations, a recent arrival in human history, a "practical affair" in which citizens accept moral and legal norms in return for a dependable security and commercial framework (Pfaff 1994, 23).

But, Pfaff says, "[n]ationalism, of course, is intrinsically absurd" (Pfaff 1994, 17), and "has consistently overridden principles of international solidarity and political or religious universalism" (Pfaff 1994, 24). The "traumas of modernization" in the nineteenth century "left national attachment as the principal surviving factor in an individual's sense of identity" (Pfaff 1994, 43–44). While efforts toward what Pfaff calls an "inadvertent commonwealth" have followed the "evil in twentieth-century history," and may be viewed as some progress, it must be remembered that "man as such does not grow better. He is free. He remains the beast/angel Pascal called him, a chaos, contradiction, prodigy. He progresses only by recognizing his nature, his misery together with his sublime possibility. A politics has to be built on that" (Pfaff 1994, 238). Which, when applied to security, nicely shows why saving cities and everything that goes with them now depends on self-selected individuals.

After surveying the growth of nationalism, history professor Hans Kohn concluded that "nationalism is a deeply divisive force" that "hardly helps to promote cooperation among people at the very time when for technological and economic reasons they grow more and more interdependent" (Kohn 1955, 90).

Kohn's book includes twenty-four "readings" on nationalism. Reading no. 8 is from an essay by British historian Lord Acton (1834–1903) criticizing Joseph Mazzini's concept of nationality. Acton asserts that "[t]he theory of nationality, therefore, is a retrograde step in history" (Kohn 1955, 125), because even a state that accommodates distinct groups without oppressing them "labours to neutralize, to absorb, or to expel them [and] destroys its own vitality. . . . Its course will be marked with material as well as moral ruin, in order that a new invention may prevail over the works of God and the interests of mankind" (Kohn 1955, 125).

Another scholar of nationalism, Elie Kedourie, criticizes Kant's *Perpetual Peace* for holding that all states should become republics. Only "arbitrariness, lawlessness, and violence on a stupendous scale" can follow such attempts to "wipe the canvas clean" (Kedourie 1993, xiv).

Kedourie concludes, "[t]he attempts to refashion so much of the world on national lines has not led to greater peace and stability." On the contrary, "it has created new conflicts, excerbated tensions, and brought catastrophe to number-less people innocent of all politics" (Kedourie 1993, 133–34). Interestingly for my thesis that citizens should empower them-selves through their cities, Kedourie notes that the rise of nationalism often undermined the security of urban groups by subordinating their civilization and culture to a national will (Kedourie 1993, 123–24).

Nations defend their sovereignties and resist transferring or sharing power. But war profiteers buy national governments, perpetuate reliance on military solutions, and deprive popula-tions of the shield of enforced law. To the extent that such inter-est groups control policy, they defeat the fond expectation of citizens that their nation is theirs. On the other hand, the rela-tionships among federal, state, and municipal layers of gov-ernment work within the United States, continuously adjusted through judicial and political interpretations. Why should supra-national federalism prove less practical?

Power

Citizens in a democracy must be conscious power holders. Democracy, and the law that democracy must command, is illu-sory, transitory, or both to the extent that individual citizens do not consciously exercise power. To confound democracy with nation instead of people, and power with nation instead of peo-ple, risks it all.

To appreciate the power shifts, imagine human power, like the atoms of the universe, as a fixed quantity, endlessly experi-encing assembly and fragmentation. Power's ubiquity and con-stant mass means that power not held by A will always be held by B or C, or B and C together. A vacuum never exists. Every particle not in my hands is in someone else's.

Acts of citizenship—voting, political organizing, lobbying, protesting, and channeling money—exercise power. Lacking a Machiavelli to instruct us about power, we don't think of it in a Machiavellian way. Most, not aspiring to power, fail to see that their responsibility is not just to allocate power but to obtain and use it, and that the growth or decline of democracy rests with a willingness to do so. To decline to do more than vote is an act of nullification. In the United States, everyman's avocation has decayed into lifestyle—elections as entertainment, popularity contests, and opinion polls, and in the case of corporate interests that buy government to suit their needs, as commodities.

Mikhail Gorbachev concludes that "[p]olitical power must spread down to the people by means of decentralization of power and enhancement of the role of local self-government" (Gorbachev 2000, 264).

For any who doubt the necessity to rebuild democracy from the community level, consider that, while violence is the curse of our age and may prove the terminator of all ages, and democracy is the nonviolent way to contest for power, too few engage in the contest to pry the acolytes of military solutions from the levers of control. Most Americans content themselves with a tepid election day ratification of foregone conclusions. The occasional advent of a genuine change agent like Barack Obama too often is seized as an excuse to do even less civically, tying the change agent's hands and facilitating return of the oligarchs.

Citizens

Citizens acquire power through knowledge, conviction, and contesting for control. Those who do obtain segments of public power recognize that it is repeatedly lost and regained, and continually balanced against other forces, those of property, wealth, business, and the media. When elections are not decided by weighing issues and voting objectively, citizens are powerless. Citizens must grip a bit of government with a hostile, jealous, exclusiveness. The powers of law, taxing, police, the military— all will be possessed by someone, and if not by the many as citizens, then by the few as exploiters, because the social universe, the human community, contains a fixed amount of power, every piece eternally in contest.

Not to consider oneself a power holder as well as a power allocator denies the purposes of citizenship. We misconstrue democracy when we settle for expressing opinions with the idea that powers-that-be will respond. To express an opinion to a power holder is a faint echo of power. Power surrendered, power unused, never lapses, and ground surrendered by public disuse is occupied instantly by private interests.

Democracy

The most egregious power surrender has been of the electoral process. If an election's product will be the same no matter who wins, the election is a sham. Today, few U.S. congressional or state legislative elections involve a contest. Most incumbents are not challenged, or not challenged by anyone with a chance of winning. In August 2006 the Washington bureau chief of the *Financial Times* reported that, due to gerrymandering, only twenty of the 435 seats (5%) in the House of Representatives would prove competitive in the November 2006 elections (*Financial Times*, August 4, 2006). The 2006 and 2008 elections condemn the Bush administration far more than they commend the U.S. political system. In 2004, a more typical year, 98 percent of incumbent Congress members—all but four—won reelection. Ninety-four percent of incumbents were not even opposed that year.

About 15,000 federal and state election districts are gerrymandered so that a minority party in a district cannot win even if a reasonable number of voters evaluate issues and candidates independently in the final election. As the gerrymander renders final elections one-sided, the seat can only be contested in the majority party's primary election. Primaries fail at the task of offering a true choice because they are easily manipulated: the majority party, for instance, will run one or more ringers, or shadow candidates whose names are placed on the ballot not to contest the seat for themselves and with no expectation of winning, but to split opponents and protect the incumbent.

Former New Jersey Senator Bill Bradley concludes, "[o]ver the last twenty-five years, increased precision from computer modeling, efforts to create black districts in order to comply with the Voting Rights Act, and the natural tendency of incumbents to improve their prospects have created a House of Representatives in which barely more than 10 percent of the 435 seats are regularly contested. The effect of this is profound" (Bradley 2007, 203). He goes on to explain that in districts drawn to give incumbents lopsided majorities everything depends on small turnout primaries in which candidates, instead of building consensus among the public, "bow to the most extreme elements in their coalition" (Bradley 2007, 203).

Presidential and gubernatorial elections are little better because, with so much at stake, the major parties and those who control them, aided by the media, stifle independent thought and block departure from established wisdom and from the existing power allocation. If it takes a near total meltdown—of the economy, foreign and security policy, and the environment—to elect a competent, public-oriented president, the price is too high.

Opinion poll elections are won by persuading a majority to hold a particular set of opinions. It is a sham to masquerade the public as a power player. If policy is unaffected, public opinion is like a batch of purloined ballots, hijacked on their way for delivery to the counting hall and stuffed down a sewer. Not that elections matter when the candidates themselves are constrained by players more powerful than the voters—financing sources, slanted media, and ideological fixations—to the point that the candidates offer voters no real policy choices.

If every election presented two independently thinking candidates of integrity and sound judgment who communicated their views comprehensively rather than adulterated into sound bites, and if voters analyzed and evaluated those views, then democracy might be served by merely voting. Anyone who expects to encounter in the course of a lifetime more than one or two candidates or a handful of voters who meet these standards makes two errors. The first is to think that candidates emerge and behave as a product of conviction and career commitment rather than as protégés and agents of interest groups. The second is to think that an analytical public that might discern such candidates can emerge from a consumer-oriented, advertising-based, money-driven society.

In authentic democracy, power would shift back and forth among segments of the public. In America's pretend democracy, power is centralized, and seeming shifts prove inconsequential. People hold contradictory views about where the power lies. They want to believe that they—the public—hold the power, so they assume that those in leadership positions respond to public "opinion." But, of course, the leaders are politicians, and the public denegrates and disrespects politicians. What passes for public opinion is scattershot impression and nurtured bias. The real power holders transform intellectual civic sloth into feel-good patriotism through a combination of flattery, mythology, and spectacle.

Mikhail Gorbachev makes a similar observation as to democracies worldwide:

> Existing electoral systems by no means guarantee genuine representation for the majority in government bodies. As a result of growing abstention from voting and fragmentation of the

> vote, many parties are unable to get a sufficient percentage of
> the vote to gain a seat in parliament; thus the current parlia-
> mentary forms of government have in fact come to represent
> only a minority of the population. (Gorbachev 2000, 262)

Machiavelli notes the tendency of a republic "in tran-
quil times to make small note of men of merit," leading, he
observes, to disastrous military adventures such as the Athenian invasion of Sicily when the counsel of the ambitious Alcib-
iades was preferred over that of the public-minded Nicias
(Machiavelli 1940, 263–64). With too much wealth, Machiavelli
says, reputations are pursued for private rather than the public good. Wealth leads to reputation and influence becoming
dependent on private means instead of being "open to every
citizen" (Machiavelli 1940, 494).

Wealth also erodes the quality of deliberative assemblies
because it multiplies ambitions and jealousies, leading to rejec-
tion of superior leaders, who are resented, and to giving preference "to what is suggested by men who are more desirous
of pleasing the masses than of promoting the general good"
(Machiavelli 1940, 354). Machiavelli recommends two remedies:
first, "keep the citizens poor," and second, "so organize for war
as to be ever prepared for it, and always to have need of men of
merit" (Machiavelli 1940, 354). Note, however, that Machiavelli
does not recommend waging war.

Let us recall why species preservation, or at least civilization preservation, may depend on recasting democracy.
Sixty-five years into the nuclear age, no effective alternative to
national WMD competition has been advocated by any presidential candidate. Even a Barack Obama, for all the promise he held
as his term began, dared not mount this as a leading campaign
issue. Almost no federal or state legislator, or municipal or
county office holder has ever taken serious issue with the WMD
arms race. Global prohibition of creating, storing, and selling

WMD is within our capability, but we decline to seek a universal rule, to make it law, because we are told that it would intrude on American sovereignty and security. We rely on threats and sanctions to curtail proliferation, which fuels chauvinist hostility. (While these chapters make more of a point about the nuclear threat, WMD embraces biological and chemical weapons as well.)

For any who might agree that elections are opinion polls at best, who would like to allocate to effective international institutions the power to prevent nuclear catastrophe at the hands of terrorists, consider that what remains of citizen power is found in municipalities. This power is potentially vast because municipalities are numerous, intimate with individuals, and yet globally dispersed. The gerrymander is less likely to foreclose entry. Local media is more accessible. Citizen organizations can exercise decisive influence.

Holders of right and left political views can find common ground in a commitment to strengthen democracy. In *The Coming Anarchy*, Robert Kaplan, whose remarkable ballyhooing of war we shall note in a later chapter, despairs of efforts to establish democracy in countries that lack a middle class and provides discouraging examples (like Sudan) observed during his journalistic career. He points to the enlarging sphere of global corporate power in the U.S. and abroad as well as to the influence of technology and those in control of it as further counterdemocratic developments, even where a strong middle class is evident. "While we preach our version of democracy abroad, it slips away from us at home" (Kaplan 2001, 83). He thinks America is headed toward oligarchy with increasing power in the hands of corporations and less in those of citizens.

> Democratic governance, at the federal, state, and local levels, goes on. But its ability to affect our lives is limited. The

> growing piles of our material possessions make personal life more complex and leave less time for communal matters. And as communities become liberated from geography, as well as more specialized culturally and electronically, they will increasingly fall outside the realm of traditional governance. Democracy loses meaning if both rulers and ruled cease to be part of a community tied to a specific territory. In this historical transition phase, lasting perhaps a century or more, in which globalization has begun but is not complete and loyalties are highly confused, civil society will be harder to maintain. How and when we vote during the next hundred years may be a minor detail for historians. (Kaplan 2001, 86–87)

Precisely. As communities—that is, cities and towns—are liberated from their geographical territory, they jointly become targets, the putative victims of "advanced" technological warfare. So let us make something of this. If we are intelligent, free, and empowered, let us invent.

Kaplan sees the negative side but imagines no way to correct it or compensate for it:

> The last thing America needs is more voters—particularly badly educated and alienated ones—with a passion for politics. . . . The masses avoid important national and international news because much of it is tragic. . . . This willingness to give up self and responsibility is the *sine qua non* for tyranny. . . . An elite with little loyalty to the state and a mass society fond of gladiator entertainments form a society in which corporate Leviathans rule and democracy is hollow. (Kaplan 2001, 89–93)

The word *masses* is a giveaway. Kaplan never says that the masses are not capable of responsible citizenship, and maybe he does not think that. Maybe becoming part of the masses is a choice, even if not a conscious choice. However, because he offers no solutions, I suspect that he thinks they (we) are indeed not capable. We shall return to this critical question of citizen quality and varying perceptions of it.

Democracy is how a public can control the rules. By *public* I mean citizens too numerous, widespread, and fluid for control by private parties. Now that global destruction is within the reach, or soon to be within the reach, of undeterrable, irresponsible parties, the public and the rules for governing the public—or at least those that govern security—together with the democracy through which the rules must be controlled, must achieve global reach.

Law

It builds on sand to recommend democracy for nations without recommending democratically accountable international law that can ensure the independence of those nations and provide the human rights protections needed to avoid civil war.

This fundamental necessity to make law's jurisdiction and democracy's control coterminous both within and between nations eludes the imagination of most Americans. The United States wants to impose both security rules and democracy on other nations without reference to any rules to which it will itself submit. That other peoples will not accept rules imposed by another nation, any more than Americans will, seems beyond comprehension.

The Disconnect Goes Global

International trade regulation illustrates the indispensable role of democratically grounded international law for the purpose of eliminating WMD. The manufacture and trading of weapons, inspections that verify arms limitations, and peacekeeping all necessitate rules that are democratically adopted and enforced. If the U.S. government continues to retard the development of international law, if activists make the mistake of objecting to all international regulation rather than advocating its democratic control, and with no proposals on the table for achieving a global regime of democratically accountable enforced law, we are left with an ever more dangerous state of anarchy.

The United States rejects international law in the fields of criminal justice, war prevention, human rights, trade, investment regulation, environmental protection, and the law of war according to a British scholar of international law, Philippe Sands. Examining World Trade Organization law, for example, Sands notes that when WTO rules negated progress under American law in environmental protection and employee health, safety, and economic safeguards, a popular backlash ensued, exemplified by the 1999 anti-WTO demonstrations in Seattle (Sands 2005, 16). He concludes, "democratic deficit is inherent in all modern international lawmaking, but is especially pronounced in the field of trade. If it is not addressed, serious political discord is bound to arise" (Sands 2005, 103).

Richard Bellamy and R. J. Barry Jones, in their essay "Globalization and Democracy: An Afterword," conclude that "[f]aith in democracy usually goes hand-in-hand with faith in the elites" (Bellamy and Jones 2000, 200). By elites in the political rather than the economic or social context, they mean those who choose to be the political operatives, who are relied on "to reduce the agenda to manageable proportions," who serve as the "political class" (Bellamy and Jones 2000, 200). One can read this as cynicism that downgrades democracy's luster, or, as I read it, the opportunity to reconfigure democracy by becoming a political operative, part of this elite. In other words, let us not accept the saw "my vote does not count" because, while that may be nearly true by magnitude, the only way for it to be effectively true is to rest content as a mere voter.

Richard Falk contributes to *Global Democracy: Key Debates* an essay, "Global Civil Society and the Democratic Prospect." Falk insists that global civil society can best achieve democratic empowerment by "reconnecting politics with moral purpose and values, which calls attention to the moral emptiness of neo-liberalism, consumerism, and most forms of secularism" (Falk 2000, 171). This approach will also "weaken the political appeal of resurgent organized religion while at the same time acknowl-edging the relevance of moral purpose and spiritual concerns to the renewal of progressive politics" (Falk 2000, 171).

For the countries in which it has been adopted, democracy has seemed like the culmination of political striving and an appropriate model to impose on others, as the United States did in Japan in 1945 (where the model proved feasible) or in Iraq today (where it may not). Where fanaticism, ethnic or religious pluralism, and an unstable economic and educational platform deliver a country's political course to idealogues, tyrants, or deranged leaders, even the best of democratic constitutions and a cadre of sincere advocates may prove insufficient. Contempo-rary complexities and WMD dangers limit the effectiveness of democracy, when it is constricted by national borders, to shield people and preserve civilization.

Given the geographic dispersion of polyglot ideological dif-ferences and disagreements among nations that are ill-equipped to resolve such differences politically as well as the organiza-tional advantages that computer technology gives to terror-ists who seek to command WMD, a limited tragedy like civil war could trigger global catastrophe. Hence, law must become global, and the democracy adequate to make it accountable must be global as well. Philippe Sands asks, "If participatory democracy is relevant to the national levels of governments, then why should it not also apply at the international level, where so many decisions which affect people's lives are now being taken" (Sands 2005, 18).

Bellamy and Jones note, as others have, that steps toward global democracy through the UN are futile because, as a "club of states," the UN's institutions cannot serve nonstate interests.

Advocates of democracy at the global level will have to find "alternative sources of power, a sense of community, and a suitable founding moment" (Bellamy and Jones 2000, 211). They cite the European Union as an environment for experimenting with democratic governance without creating transnational government. "In sum," they write, "the possibility of global democracy lies in new forms of governance, modifying and complementing but not replacing, old forms of government" (Bellamy and Jones 2000, 214).

Columbia University professor José E. Alvarez, the 2006-07 president of the American Society of International Law, identified the many ways in which international trade, dispute settlement, judicial, and other rule-making organizations are creating law. They expand the norms or customary law that become enforceable notwithstanding the absence of any treaty to which a nation might have adhered, as to which we shall have more to say in a later chapter. The United Nations General Assembly, Alvarez notes, "cross-references" resolutions by calling on nations to adopt the substance of the resolutions in their domestic law, or to include in nationally collected statistics and reports information regarding the substance of the resolution, thus multiplying the impact. As an example, the UN Convention on the Law of the Sea has adopted navigational rules, pollution controls, and other regulations that, by becoming norms, eventually bind nonsigners of the treaty. The World Bank, International Civil Aviation Organization, International Labor Organization, and UN Security Council all have cross-referenced, according to Alvarez, and have generated negotiation and adoption of numerous treaties.

Cross-border, democratic action will begin to redress the disconnect when cities and towns elect representatives to make common cause with other threatened urban populations.

On election day [of the 1952 presidential election], however, New Mexico was not so hospitable. [Adlai] Stevenson lost the state by a big vote, but that was hardly a surprise to me because he conducted the campaign in our state with the same indifference to popular preferences that he showed elsewhere. New Mexico had developed a significant atomic energy industry—though few people knew then how genuinely important it was to the manufacture of nuclear weapons. Stevenson, with his thoughtful approach to atomic weaponry, simply would not offer New Mexicans the assurances they wanted to hear that their industry would stay alive. I know that Stevenson remained silent on this matter because he had a profound commitment to disarmament and would not resort to deception to collect a few votes. But the Sandia Corporation, which was the heart of the new industrial complex, was important to New Mexico and the people were more concerned about their jobs than Adlai Stevenson's integrity. For better or for worse, this concern is what politics is all about—and this same factor, multiplied may times over throughout the country, was fundamental to Stevenson's loss of the election. (Anderson 1970, 120)

—Senator Clinton P. Anderson

PART IV

RESOURCES

If we are to prefer orderly governance and a secure future to contests for prizes of violence and the phantom championship of world dominance that those contests imply, then strategies are required that enable the millions to share the power that nation states reserve for the few. Call it democracy updated or democracy expanded, but recognize that it necessitates every bit as desperate a power struggle as that which surrounds the throne of violence, demanding as much innovation, invention, and work as that which creates ever deadlier bombs and missiles. Urban ballots against the war system will be a David-and-Goliath battle, but remember who won.

Memorandum to President Kennedy, December 8, 1961

Ten or eleven votes have made us appear to be against nuclear disarmament, against the cessation of nuclear testing except on our terms, against free zones, against undertakings by non-nuclear states not to acquire nuclear weapons and even against an inquiry on the subject, and against an African effort to keep nuclear weapons out of the African continent. Looked at from the other point of view, we appear to be fighting for the use of nuclear weapons, for their proliferation, and for the possibility of their employment in any continent or area.

Of course, this "image" of the United States is grossly inaccurate. Nevertheless, it is now rather widely shared by African and Asian delegates, and even some Latin American delegates have voted as if they gave it at least some credence. The Soviet bloc have been quick to exploit our voting record, and, of course, have voted for most all of these resolutions. Their voting record on these popular issues does not reveal their shamelss hypocrisy, and I suspect the Soviet propaganda machine is making good use of the record. (Stevenson 1979, 171–72)

—Adlai E. Stevenson, United States ambassador to the United Nations, 1961–1965

CHAPTER 11

Welfare Queen and Patriot King: Take the Impediments Back to the Neighborhood

Recall the demand for a means test to get idle welfare mothers off the dole. If Welfare Queen—a woman who could support herself and children but chose not to—existed, now we have her national security counterpart, Patriot King—my shorthand for a variety of business, political, media, and academic people who find more reasons to arm, threaten, and attack than to build bridges, remove incentives to violence, and enforce peace—luxuriating on the war dole, his tax returns hedged with deductions for depreciation, travel, entertainment, and gigantic salaries. He (and she) shares the bounty with employees, plus the many who thrill to war gaming, the awe of technoweapons, war adventure, war pathos, war pride, and primordial feelings about justice, revenge, hatred, and triumph.

For fun and profit, this war child drags us all into his private world, and we allow him to enlarge and articulate it as an economy, way of life, entertainment center, and house of faith. Welfare Queen serves as a target, an alleged financial drag on Patriot King's glory. Following his wreckage on the poor and profiteering from government contracts and patriotic ballyhoo, Patriot King attacks environmental control, sound energy policy, and more, on the grounds that they rely on too much government. A hundred thousand or half million Iraqi civilian deaths, take your pick, and four thousand U.S. service deaths barely hint at the nuclear hell toward which Patriot King propels us.

With my apologies for a degree of oversimplification, let us sort out some of the themes about security policy to suggest how threadbare our dialogue about the supreme issue of the day really is.

The glory and curse of humanity is to exploit everything within reach, to excessively enrich and dangerously empower feckless progeny, and to convert every experience—war, sex, nourishment, learning—into entertainment, whether to enhance and beautify or to trivialize and wreak havoc. With the intelligence that facilitates this exploitation, we build realms of knowledge, manipulate resources, imagine, invent, and so forth. Despite our well-evidenced capacity to chart a rational course, we possess no natural inclination, no instinct, to do so. Call it free will or call it stupidity, when we act against a secure future, we act neither wisely nor rationally. Laziness substitutes morality and religion for intelligence.

Democracy is supposed to expand horizons. Endowed with the power and the opportunity, people are expected to consult together, analyze, and learn. So that there would be no mistake about the rationality that self-government would demand, religion was excluded from the consulting and deciding arena.

To restate my main thesis: security hangs upon finding, in multiple nations, an arena for discrediting militaristic security policies and substituting policies predicated on law enforcement that prevents war.

If preventing war were in fact a national policy, a plan for how to achieve it would be a plank in every party platform and in the platform of every candidate for national—and increasingly, one would hope, state and local—offices. There would be conservative plans, liberal plans, radical plans as determinedly advanced as positions on the economy, taxes, health care, and education.

To discredit war's pervasive acceptability, the seeming contradiction of being equipped to prevail if war becomes unavoidable, and ensuring that it will not prove unavoidable, has to be unraveled. Part of the persuasion must be grounded in the dependability of international military forces sent in the capacity of rule-making, adjudication, and policing progressively to reduce occasions for armed conflict.

It is difficult to say which has been the more discouraging—the Reagan/Bush/Bush quarter-century of discrediting the United Nations (withholding dues, appointing an ambassador like John Bolton), or the opposition party's failure to keep the vision of an effective UN, or any alternative vision of pursuing security other than military might, before the public.

But We Already Are Preventing War

One impediment is the widespread mistaken belief that preventing war already is the policy of this nation and its friends, especially other democracies. The public thinks "everyone" wants peace, that the nations do prefer peace to war, and when nations engage in war it is from necessity or mistaken judgment, an error to be corrected. Political action becomes an exercise in trying to persuade national governments, usually after the fact, to correct operating decisions rather than determine policy.

But War Is Good

The fact is that the war system is grounded on a conviction that war is a natural, healthy human pursuit, and that national policy should be directed not to preventing but to winning wars. Consider another of Samuel Huntington's recommended readings, Kaplan's *The Coming Anarchy*.*

In his last chapter, "The Dangers of Peace," Kaplan, a journalist, author, and fellow at the New America Foundation, writes that

> Peace, as a primary goal, is dangerous because it implies that
> you will sacrifice any principle for the sake of it. A long period
> of peace in an advanced technological society like ours could
> lead to great evils, and the ideal of a world permanently at
> peace and governed benignly by a world organization is not an
> optimistic view of the future but a dark one. (Kaplan 2001, 169)

You have to truly value war to insist that pursuing peace necessitates sacrificing other principles of value, and to insist that world order and democratic control are incompatible. Kaplan goes on to claim, after noting that the Cold War was close to utopia, that enemies serve to define your own values like freedom and prosperity, and that peace, because it is pleasurable, leads to a preoccupation with presentness at the cost of losing the past and disregarding the future.

Kaplan also writes, "Whereas war leads to a respect for large, progressive government, peace creates an institutional void filled by, among other things, entertainment-oriented corporations." Furthermore, "A long domestic peace would rear up leaders with no tragic historical memory, and thus little wisdom. . . . [P]ermanent peace, with its worship of entertainment

---

* Huntington's endorsement, printed in a collection of endorsements on pages before the title page, reads: "Filled with penetrating insight into the grim realities of today's world. Kaplan vividly describes conflicts and contradictions which too many policy makers and scholars attempt to ignore."

and convenience, will produce ever-shallower leaders" (Kaplan 2001, 174–75, 183).

Kaplan rushes, of course, to discredit the United Nations, which "represents not just the hopes but more accurately the illusions of millions of people, from those in Third World villages to university liberal arts departments, who want to escape from the historical cycle of war and power politics" (Kaplan 2001, 177). No clue is offered as to why he thinks you cannot have politics without war, although he seems to contradict the thought when he says that "a really politically muscular international organization is undesirable" (Kaplan 2001, 176).

Since my book advocates a power struggle, I hope it helps give the lie to this Kaplan assertion about peace seekers: "The UN bureaucracy, along with others who seek a peaceful world, worship consensus" (Kaplan 2001, 178).

Pacifism? Good, Within Limits

I have served in the military and am no pacifist, but I readily endorse five central beliefs that seem to me implicit in pacifism: (a) fighting provokes more violence than it ends and kills more people than would be slaughtered if they did not defend themselves; (b) the world is too large for an unresisted aggressor to govern, so passive resistance would prevail in the end; (c) nonviolent forms of resistence would prevent much of the slaughter; (d) in the absence of planned, announced willingness to wage war, greater effort would be made to prevent war, because the delusion would be shed that arming accomplishes anything but stimulating arms competition and ultimately the use of arms; (e) to suspend arms manufacture would knock the props from under the collateral stimulations and excuses for war, like weapons profiteering, uncritical patriotism, demonizing opponents, seeking revenge, and contingency preparations that tend to make the feared contingency come true.

The only inaccurate dimension of such beliefs is that they leave too much to chance. Foreclosing the dangers of war requires a proactive stance. A well-conceived alternative organization of authority would protect us more than simply terminating the stimulants of war, essential though termination may be. Security necessitates a system as much as war requires a system. A security system would deploy a regime of law, enforced by fully as comprehensive an arrangement of administration, adjudication, and force as characterizes domestic law. Such arrangement would preclude a competing war system.

Humans? Not Good Enough

Lack of confidence in human capacity is a primary obstacle to change. War system apologists like Robert Kaplan and peace advocates alike lack such confidence. The one says that the public is incapable of imposing and maintaining order, a task for which only armed forces will suffice. The other tends to think that the mere absence of armed forces would bring about peace.

War is as mutable as most human practices. It has been used for myriad purposes, has involved varying portions of populations, and has meant different things to different people. To understand this is a key to security, because it contradicts the inevitability with which many cloak war, and it contradicts the sense that security from war requires total abstinence. Those who insist that character, spirit, courage, or any of a number of other positive attributes deteriorate if one renounces war should be asked, "Well, if we could just have little wars, would you go that far with us?" Because those who hanker to honor war needn't worry about abstinence. Global and regional peacekeeping forces, in our hoped-for safer world, will require law enforcement, and there will be plenty of military career opportunities and weapons profits to boot. Would-be dictators and violence-prone agitators, ideological fanatics, religious nuts, and persecutors of minorities will always be available. Some of these will have to be beaten down or killed, or dragged to law courts so that their cases may be tried through law instead of guns.

Among the criticisms that war-system stalwarts will aim at our ideas will be disparagement of the capacity of urban voters. The word urban conjures poor, inner city, drop out, and a few other supposed disabilities. My responses are three:

1. By urban I mean to include suburbanites and villagers, essentially everyone with a local government that can be enlisted.

2. Far too many elite university graduates are at the heart of the war system, and prove no dependable resource for security.

3. If urban dwellers are not adequately trained for citizenship, perhaps placing security reliance on them will increase the motivation to give them a first-rate education, in terms of teacher quality, money spent, and seriousness of the curriculum.

Make Democracy Deliver

Faced with nuclear chaos delivered by terrorist purveyors of hatred, we must make democracy deliver on its promise. The place to start is in neighborhoods. We will know we are making progress when Patriot King or his stand-ins and toadies show up, which they will do if we get to the heart of the matter. When a few cities and towns here and abroad begin to undermine the war system and pressure their nations to replace it with international peace enforcement, opponents of peace enforcement will be met face to face. Some will be war veterans convinced that military solutions are the only solutions to the problem of terrorism; some will be low-information voters convinced that we are ceding U.S. independence to a world dictatorship; some will be Patriot King's sycophants from business, finance, the media, the clergy, or the military. Some will wave the flag and extol every value but green power and intact flesh and blood. They will be very convincing on the intangible values that separate peoples, and they will put to the test the power of social invention and the value of love and human kindness.

I also look forward to seeing the antiwar activists who have invited me to so many seminars, teach-ins, speeches, and vigils where the only people I ever met were like-minded and where voices of opposition never ventured and no strategy was devised to either entice or force our opponents to confer—because confer with them we must. Where there is no opposition, there can be little discipline of thought, and devising solid, feasible alternatives to the policies to which we object becomes immeasurably harder.

The Goal of Informed Debate

What shall we decide in our neighborhoods? We shall decide that city hall and town hall are near enough that we may exert influence over them, and that if the goal of empowering accountable elected representatives is to impose enforced security law on all nations and peoples, the initial elections must be municipal elections. On the way to deciding whether this conclusion is a realistic goal, reflect that the neighborhood is the only level at which authentic citizen debate ever takes place. We assign the national government too many roles—as right-wing politicians hypocritically argue—and the city and town too few, although when the right says government is too big, and that the national government has too many roles, they really want the roles to disappear altogether. They count on civic laziness to inhibit reconstituting locally the functions they have stripped from the national government. They would "liberate" us all from the burden of solving our joint problems in the only way they can be solved, which is jointly, through government.

I want a security debate in my neighborhood: first, to marshal the intelligence, support, and understanding of individuals to save their civilization; second, to nail nation-state security derelictions high on the pole; and third, to explore imposing enforced security law on nations, corporations, and agents of violence.

Some folks from Los Angeles ought to ask Mayor Antonio Villaraigosa, who committed L.A. to the Kyoto Protocol as soon as he took office (Garrahan 2008), and some folks from Tokyo ought to ask Governor Shintaro Ishihara, Tokyo's governor, who imposed Japan's first cap-and-trade carbon emissions plan (Sable 2008), each to ask Mayor Mohammad-Bagher Qalibaf of Teheran for the names and addresses of Teheran's 380 neighborhood chairs and citizen council chairs (Bozorgmehir 2008).

I also want neighborhood debate because, in large cities, elections to regional and global municipal assemblies can best be organized initially in neighborhoods. Thousands of city districts are cohesive enough to act as units within their municipal or metropolitan universe. During the first year or two, as a few municipally elected officials create the framework for the security congress and begin to place the election of global representatives on the municipal ballot, the only test for the level of participation should be civic cohesion. Wherever and however people can unite for security, they should do so.

Cities and towns are where fellow citizens can be talked with, and newspapers, radio, and television can be easily accessed. In local politics, sincerity and judgment must be validated and attention earned. Once earned, tens of thousands of attainable offices exist, each carrying a segment of power that, if marshaled, can harness the will of citizens to influence the White House and Congress.

Some might argue that debate splinters opinion when the nation needs cohesion and relief from the culture wars. Security, they will say, rests on gathered and focused patriotism, on a mindset that a wider focus would weaken. How can a president faced with divisions command sacrifice from citizens who carry emotional commitments to homelands of their forebears and other magnets of affection or interest that rival commitment to nation and flag?

The Goal of Unity

Authentic unity can only follow informed debate, which is the last thing that Americans have today. We do very well at citizenship responsibility in areas where we are obviously affected—parents on behalf of their schoolchildren, outdoor enthusiasts over parks, and (more recently) environmentalists over global warming. By coalescing, some of these efforts will transform participants as they combine forces, from lobbyists to power seekers. In the next chapter, we shall look more closely at how public forums might be employed to enhance security.

To insist on local debate and decision-making does not in the least discount the present federal system. To the contrary, federalism will open the door to exploring the supranational level that must be fashioned to serve at once all nations and peoples. Global federalism is the essential next step—not global federation, but federalism, which is cooperation to achieve what no nation can achieve alone. Yet taking this step is thwarted by the disillusionment of many at the failure to utilize national and state governments for their best and highest purposes. Many insist that less government is called for just when events call for coordination, control, and management.

Anyone who thinks municipal involvement in foreign and security policy would be futile or dangerous should reflect on how Muslim and Christian ideologues turn issue-based political disagreements into religious wars. This tactic "localizes" global issues far more than do this book's proposals to involve cities and towns in security strategy. A religious touchstone for global issues imposes a personal, individual test in place of what ought to be a judgment of what is best for all. The times call for expanding our intellectual grasp and becoming world citizens, but the trend is to crawl into a stone hut of elemental feelings.

The infusion of religion into policy debate is occasioned by churches offering forums where parishioners find an outlet for their sense of a world flying apart. Ill-chosen to the extent that they impose nonrational analysis on problems that only reason can resolve, churches fill a vacuum. A near-monopoly to comment on the mounting risks of nuclear disaster has been given to evangelical television preachers who insist it is the inevitable playing out of Biblical prophecies of the rapture. Municipal involvement in security and foreign policy would reclaim public policy for democratic decision-making.

Those Intangible Values That Separate Us
Consider the case of the Bush administration's deputy undersecretary of defense, Lt. Gen. William G. Boykin, who was ordered to apologize after the public learned that he attended twenty-three religious events in uniform and exhorted parishioners to battle Satan in the guise of Islamic militancy and said that God had put President Bush in the White House (*New York Times*, August 20, 2004). Watch Oliver North when Fox News features his religion-laced denunciations of Islamic militant attacks on Israel. Listen to preachers Pat Robertson and Jack Van Impe raving that Israel is the seat of a religious war foretold in the Book of Revelations and by Old Testament prophets. In Iran, fundamentalists have been calling the United States the Great Satan for quite a while.

The political right started gathering power through school board elections thirty years ago. While the right began to control the dialogue, liberals were content to intellectualize about what presidents ought to do, as if the voters' job were to think up policy directives for pedestrian politicians.

Attention to Real Substance Leads to Security

By misconstruing the federal system, we have lost track of governing essentials. The founding states needed a central government, but in defining its mission the authors of the Constitution hardly intended to belittle essential citizenship tasks. Our reverence for the Constitution perhaps leads to taking the individual's essential role too much for granted. To vote once in four years in presidential elections, which is about all that most do, is so ephemeral that to pretend that it exercises freedom is delusional. As civic control over what matters shrinks, confidence in the system sags. A rare populist victory like that in 2008 translates to overreliance on the anointed victor instead of commitment to capitalize on an opportunity and perpetuate the civic endeavor.

Global security ought to be the first target for community involvement. Anyone who thinks that local communities already have a full plate of responsibilities should consider what else cries for attention that, if given, would replenish Americans' political influence and power. As the fiscally disadvantaged level of government, municipalities should document for their residents why and how the federal and state governments divide the hodgepodge of tax exactions and exemptions, take the lion's share through income taxes, and play favorites in both the exactions and redistributions. Municipalities should tell residents every year the percentage of tax dollars spent at each level of government and for what purposes. They should let every household compare its direct and indirect tax contribution with what the richest and poorest Americans pay and business pays.

It is pretense to suppose the public controls goal priorities if most people neither understand nor act upon resource allocation. In theory, we evaluate the policies and fairness of each levy, and cast informed votes for candidates at three levels. In practice, most Americans haven't a clue whether taxes at any level are an appropriate size or properly spent, or who the ultimate beneficiaries are. All of these essential functions belong to democratic citizens. To reclaim them, one has to start at a level of practical effectiveness.

Remember that 9/11 struck at a city, and reflect upon subjects that are usually thought beyond the purview and competence of municipal government, but that increasingly impact people precisely at the municipal level.

1. The federal budget affects local tax rates by dictating the amount of resources available for matters closest to home: schools, police, and health care.

2. Few Americans are well informed or dispassionately informed about foreign policy and security issues, notwithstanding historically unparalleled opportunities to obtain information and despite the mortal consequences of making unsound decisions. This state of affairs leaves decision-making to the self-interested. The manipulated, biased public that Americans have become can be blamed first on public schools, where responsibility lies for creating an electorate that knows how to seek out and analyze information. Even if we write off public schools as hopelessly inept at the preparation of an active and prepared citizenry (which I, a former school committee member, do not), municipalities remain positioned to invent means for mutually engaging people in the supreme issues of war and peace.

3. Environmental issues are now by definition global issues, just as communication resources make feasible a virtual global town meeting. The planet's habitability is a universal issue. Consensus on protection against the impacts of climate change; environmental poisoning; and diminishing resources in our oceans, forests, and agricultural land awaits the spread of awareness. These issues cry for

remedies that national agendas neglect to produce, over-
shadowed as remedies are by counterproductive efforts
to stimulate economies, reward politically connected
exploiters, and generate employment.

4. In the nuclear age, to exploit and subjugate people any-
   where for the benefit of other people; to tolerate or deem
   inevitable religious and ethnic feuds; or to surrender policy formation to businesses, lobbyists, ideologues, and
   political opportunists carries universal peril.

5. International institutions are permanently installed in
   the panoply of power wielders. Sometimes competing
   with national governments for policy control, sometimes
   the tacit allies of national governments, sometimes their
   unacknowledged agents, they can prevent war, foment
   war, override national law, correct injustice, and impose
   injustice. Ways to make them accountable to public welfare have yet to be devised.

6. A responsible president needs a better means than Oval
   Office television speeches and rigged press conferences
   to inform the public and generate consensus-building
   debate.

In all these areas, municipalities could play the role of information middleman and policy-formation facilitator. Every local
officeholder and, more to the point, every citizen as a municipal resident is in a position to urge the local media to publicize
statements illuminating the connection between the shortfall of
resources for municipal services and the counterproductive elements of the military budget, with reference to how real security might be achieved.

Machiavelli placed more reliance on the people than on the
prince:

> I say that the people are more prudent and stable, and have better judgment than a prince; and it is not without good reason that it is said, "The voice of the people is the voice of God"; for we see popular opinion prognosticate events in such a wonderful manner that it would almost seem as if the people had some occult virtue, which enables them to foresee the good and the evil. . . . We also see that in the election of their magistrates they make far better choice than princes; and no people will ever be persuaded to elect a man of infamous character and corrupt habits to any post of dignity, to which a prince is easily influenced in a thousand different ways. (Machiavelli 1940, 263–64)

We the people are amazingly multitalented. Once a problem gets our attention, we can fix it. Security is today's problem, and security commands us to master diversity and scarcity and fair allocation. Let us consider how to rivet one another's attention to our social tasks so that dependable security will get addressed.

Why has the United States been responsible for the majority of the actions that have set the rate and scale of the arms race? Why have we led the entire world in this mad rush toward the ultimate absurdity?

The reason is not that our leaders have been less sensitive to the dangers of the arms race, it is not that our leaders are less wise, it is not that we are more aggressive or less concerned about the dangers to the rest of mankind. Rather, the reasons are that we are richer and more powerful, that our science and technology are more dynamic, that we generate more ideas of all kinds. For these very reasons, we can and must take the lead in cooling the arms race, in putting the genie back into the bottle, in inducing the rest of the world to move in the direction of arms control, disarmament and sanity.

Just as our unilateral actions were in large part responsible for the current dangerous state of affairs, we must expect that unilateral moves on our part will be necessary if we are ever to get the whole process reversed. (York 1970, 238–39)

—Herbert York, Manhattan Project participant; first director of the Lawrence Livermore National Laboratory; director of defense research and engineering under Presidents Eisenhower and Kennedy; ambassador to the Comprehensive Test Ban negotiations, 1979–1981

CHAPTER 12

City and World Forums

The mock communication depicted in the media—Sean Hannity berating guests, viewers calling in to Larry King, newspaper readers writing letters to the editor—in fact just mimics discussion. Sitting at home, the public only imagines that it participates. Without the lubricant of real discussion, the backgrounds and biases of the imaginary participants congeal into antagonistic blocks. Neither Hannity nor King generate engagement or challenge preconceptions. They cannot mold a common will. Any action they stimulate is haphazard.

A fully realized democracy would run on discussions that entwine millions who are aware of their opinions and reasons for them, open to challenge, eager for facts, competitive but tolerant. Even when discussion falls short of solutions, it informs and educates, stimulates experiment. It instills mutual respect by exposing premises behind beliefs. It contributes to multinational, multicultural consensus for living by rules. To curb culture wars, reclaim the power of civic invention, reach one another and other populations despite mistrust, Americans need discussion that satisfies several criteria.

The Requisites

First, civic cohesion has to occur across social and economic lines. Discussion with the like-minded and those of similar economic and social status is but step one. That helps to confirm beliefs and to clarify, inform, and gain mutual support. Absent heartfelt challenge from people unlike oneself, though, neither underlying assumptions nor ultimate impediments are confronted. For example, one's assumption about whether war is inevitable because it is grounded in aggressive instincts emerges early in any cogent discussion about how to prevent war. Political decisions about when and if to fight wars, what kinds of conflict to prepare for, and what laws and enforcement steps are required to find security without war, relate in part to whether we possess the free will to carry a discussion back to assumptions and then forward to policy. This, and forbearance.

Second, the discussions have to lead to, or at least relate to, decisions. They need consequences, need to surmount the theoretical. If limited to what we should do or what ought to happen, discussion is just talk. Agreement on a definition of human nature is neither possible nor necessary, but the mutual recognition of the differing definitions, the assumptions behind them, and the consequences of acting upon one definition rather than another is essential to sound policymaking.

Third, public debate needs firmer positioning in the order of policymaking. Public discussion should be built into the legislative process, ahead of private interest group lobbying. Comprehensive discussion would undercut lobbying and influence-buying faster than a whole code of disclosure regulations. The routine has to be personal; vicarious participation via television will not do. Forums should be held at the neighborhood and municipal levels and wired into Congress and the state houses through a system of rotating and self-renewing discussion, or focus groups should be convened along the lines pioneered by Stanford's Center for Deliberative Democracy, which are described later in this chapter.

Fourth, people should feel obliged to join in. Declining should be conscious and temporary. We have to stay informed, respect if not accommodate contrary views, and when in the minority, persevere. Most citizens may not participate, but many, many more must take active roles in politics and policy formation than now do so. People whose experience, education, or standing in a community, neighborhood, apartment complex, or workplace make them persons to whom others listen acquire a special obligation.

A dozen generations of economic opportunity and freedom from foreign invasion and serious military defeat have afforded Americans the chance to achieve a high level of public education and civic responsibility, improve the human condition, and, above all, end war. Yet the world finds Americans selfish, fearful, and splintered. We have never put it together for the greater good, and it will take more than Barack Obama's election to change this.

Fifth, private discussions should shoulder public necessities. Public exposure confers legitimacy, endows subject matter with significance, commands respect, and broadens participation. By the same token, the process should signal compulsion, should say that not to participate is not an option, that a duty exists to be informed, to work at problems, to respect if not accommodate contrary views, to adjust to being in a minority when we are, and to work to change minds whether or not we are.

Sixth, discussions should identify time frames. Some policies and their implementation address the immediate, like the amount of taxes and appropriations for the fiscal year. Others, like a capital building plan, might involve a five- or ten-year stretch. Still others, like preventing war, have to operate in fifty- or hundred-year increments in view of the huge changes needed in how nations seek security and interact. To embark on a fifty-year project, though, would yield prompt results. Once it is understood that war is going to be prevented, never mind how long that might take, any act that retards progress becomes harder to justify. The process needs to ferret out extremism, irrationality, and self-aggrandizement, while recognizing and rewarding public-mindedness and public spirit.

One reason micro-level discourse is wanting is that it does not address the macro-level problems that we brush aside even as they confront us starkly. We talk about what is happening in the world, but as distant events, as beyond influence as the alignment of Venus and Mercury.

Americans can disagree about abortion and gay marriage but agree that nuclear attack must be prevented. If that issue were presented squarely and dialogue were generated on the requisites for avoiding nuclear attack, an essential consensus on action would emerge. Belligerent screamers disrupting Congressional health care town halls discouraged some as to the usefulness of forums for today's contentious issues. There was initial lack of control, and the media smelled circus. But we were out of practice. Raucous militancy soon discredited itself, and responsible attendees grew in number and used the discussions to master and narrow the issues.

The Choice Is Between Stifling Talk or Enabling It

Instead of remembering the tradeoffs between bigger television sets and smaller classroom sizes, or short-term energy convenience and planet habitability, or complacency and contesting security policy with weapons makers, we wind up sacrificing public to private values. Concede, if necessary to achieve public dialogue, that abortion is murder, but ask those who oppose abortion to compare the suffering of the trapped 9/11 victims with the suffering of an aborted fetus. The suffering and grief that nuclear destruction will impose demands initiatives in which the entire population engages. This is not an argument for sacrificing private values; it is a plea to insist that humanity's survival not be sacrificed either on private altars or to nationalistic jingoism. The issues that political campaigns can accommodate are limited, and the focus today should be on war and the end—all weapons that it has cast within reach of fanatic rulers and fanatic terrorists.

President Bush and Senator Kerry agreed in their 2004 presidential debates that the possibility of a terrorist nuclear attack was the most important issue facing our nation. Neither would hazard a solution. Bush, it seems, aimed to kill all the terrorists, but as the effort to do so breeds more terrorists, his "war on terror" has increased our vulnerability. Kerry, if he had an alternative, must have considered it too radical to expose to disrespectful election-time derision. In 2008, Obama and McCain proved even less specific than Kerry and Bush. Candidates, of course, never break ground that has not been seeded through public discussion, and how to prevent nuclear terrorism is little discussed where people live and work. If you asked mayors, city councilors, or aldermen to name steps to reduce the risk of a nuclear suitcase device wiping out all of their citizens, you would get a blank stare. Yet if Americans regularly engaged in meaningful dialogue about vital security issues, they would never tolerate office-seekers at any level who skim the surface.

One reason Americans do not come to grips with WMD issues is that such issues tend to be pigeonholed as too grounded in science and technology. We reserve these topics for whiz kids, effectively exempting science and technology from democratic control, even when they are central to political security and to the economic policies for which a democratic pubic nominally is responsible. There is nothing technically difficult, though, about understanding what makes terrorists want to destroy us or the mechanics of that destruction once they have a bomb.

Discussing restrictions on weapons creation need be no more arcane than a dialogue on whether to allow smoking in

restaurants. Administrations of both parties insist that nonnuclear nations continue to forego possession of nuclear weapons while holding that the United States is justified in inventing
and improving nuclear weapons in violation of the Nuclear
Non-Proliferation Treaty. In the absence of challenge, office
holders of both parties pander to an electorate for whom American character and the American system are above reproach.
To question articles of faith, anyone who runs for public office
courts defeat. A citizen who thinks and acts independently
enough to raise the issue in his hometown or neighborhood
renders his privacy vulnerable.

Consider what would make the United States submit
to the kind of international inspection process that we now
know rid Iraq of WMD before the United States invaded. How
do you keep the inspecting authority accountable? To raise
these questions invites accusations of lacking patriotism and
risking security.

Global law enforcement and global democracy must grow
together, step by step. Both democratic and nondemocratic
national governments will oppose the growth of both, and for
the same reason: reluctance to share power. Advocates of global
solutions to global problems will never elect presidents or con-
gressional/parliamentary majorities. They must achieve their
own political power at the level where it is available, in the cities and towns in which they live.

The Heart of Our Nonparticipation

What does not work in American democracy probably has not
changed over the last century, but events have made the results
worse. What does not work is the citizens, industrious in business, professions, and the community, who neglect politics and
government. Democratic citizens are supposed to follow events,
listen to one another, and make objective judgments. They cannot be coerced to mind their civic business, but at the municipal

level they could be induced to do so by giving them a stake in the power contest.

The founders differed on the question whether, given peace, prosperity, education, and the opportunity to participate in government, increasing numbers of citizens would participate. They differed on how detrimental citizen shortcomings would prove. The question must be revisited, but blind patriotism impedes the way. America is great, so the teaching goes, because America is great. No one has to do a thing—we're great.

When I was a school committee member, I used to think that the most effective path of civic endeavor was to bequeath wiser generations to the future. The politics of salvation lay with improving public education. Now our rescue time is foreshortened. We are further than ever from consensus about how to educate and what to educate for.

I glance at fellow commuters on the train, cheerful, mostly animated by dozens of conversations. Half a dozen read the *Metro Boston*, a free, sixth-grade facsimile of a tabloid newspaper. Its news reporting and analysis is summary and simplistic. A commuter or two reads the *Boston Globe* or *New York Times*. They dress informally, no suits, no jackets and ties, a sprinkling only of skirts. Lots of sneakers and sandals. A variety of facial hair—wispy goatees, bushy black beards, grey mustaches. A very few carry briefcases; many carry backpacks or laptop cases. A variety of Asian, Middle Eastern, and Indian faces are present; one or two are black. One wonders why, with this wealth of diversity, with so many in our midst who are recent residents of other lands, America's public dialogue is not vibrant, spirited, and informed.

I know from years of election campaigns that most of my fellow citizens despise politics: despise studying issues, positions, history; despise pondering the future; find no excitement or stimulation in the prospect of getting involved; and feel little responsibility for the outcome. Oddly, they are the modern counterpart of the French aristocrats in 1780—comfortable, secure, and oblivious to the march of time. The rich American business class seems a nearer analogy to French aristocrats, but rank and file Americans share the aristocratic character of a high living standard at the expense of others, secured by their preference for, or acquiescence in, militarism. By historical standards, and even in the current economic downturn, their wealth and (potential) power is huge. In fact, never has so much potential power been within the reach of so many. Insofar as they are aware of having it and think about it, they think they deserve it and won't share it beyond our borders.

Surely the quality of discourse among a democracy's citizens is something that elected officials should feel obliged to think about, and not just for the reasons I have been discussing. In her book *Terror in the Name of God*, Jessica Stern quotes British diplomat Paul Schulte, who observes that "every first-world city has a third-world one within it. . . . where residents are 'emotionally very far withdrawn from the surrounding national public space,' where dangerous and proselytizing extremist groups are likely to prey especially on individuals with 'various statuses of official citizenship and subjective identity, identification and loyalty' " (Stern 2003, 288).

In *The End of Faith*, Sam Harris blames religious tolerance for our weakness in confronting al-Qaeda's dangerous extremism: "There is no reason that our ability to sustain ourselves emotionally and spiritually cannot evolve with technology, politics, and the rest of culture" (Harris 2004, 40). He calls for discourse that is effective enough that "those standing on its fringe can come to understand the truths that it strives to articulate. This is why any sustained exercise of reason must necessarily transcend national, religious, and ethnic boundaries" (Harris 2004, 45).

In *Why Americans Hate Politics*, E. J. Dionne Jr. found that polarization on symbolic issues plus insufficient opportunity to reach common ground lay behind the public's distaste. He thought that the "pleasures of self-government" depend on escaping from the "grubby confrontation of competing interests" and addressing pragmatic solutions to problems while frankly recognizing the "healthy tension among liberty, virtue, equality, and community" (Dionne 1991, 354–55).

The one available public venue for authentic discourse is cities and towns, the only place and the only power holder that can draw out enough people and enough kinds of people, and ensure that everyone, including the media, treats the process respectfully. Suppose municipalities created Public Dialogue Commissions to which members could be elected or appointed. In larger communities, supported by paid staff, they could propose topics for inquiry, articulate choices, assemble information and provide preparatory materials, recruit participants, write reports, maintain continuity, and develop liaisons with both domestic and foreign communities as well as other levels of government.

A healthy community will already have achieved internal dialogue on local affairs, but there are few local matters that are not intertwined with the global, and that connection must be made, the connection that cements every citizen to the rest of perilously exposed humanity. We buy products from around the world, our industries export products everywhere, foreign investors support our national debt, our workers compete with labor worldwide. Americans must see that their security also depends on global discourse, for which their municipalities are the logical agents.

It used to be that police departments could handle any domestic security threat, with an occasional assist from the FBI. That time is past, but we have not yet accommodated outsize events like 9/11 in our citizen-level disclosure. We cannot quite comprehend how so outlandish an event fits in. "Mastering Uncertainty," a 2006 article in the *Financial Times* (March

24, 2006), suggested that the traditional bell curve, or Gaussian model, of risk analysis is inadequate for modern uncertainties. The bell curve predicts probable events by clustering statistical evidence. Happenings in the flat parts of the curve are statistically unlikely and therefore tend not to be prepared for, a significant insight if we are to understand why our political system has not responded effectively to the consequences of nuclear proliferation. Rather than focusing on the ordinary and dealing with exceptions as ancillaries, the authors' recommended approach "takes the exceptional as a starting point and deals with the ordinary in a subordinate manner—simply because that 'ordinary' is less consequential" (*Financial Times*, March 24, 2006). Bill Gates has so much wealth that any averaging analysis of wealth distribution is skewed if he is included. Any analysis of book sales is skewed if the Harry Potter books are included because their sales have so far outstripped those of other books. Other "wild" variables are the "size of hedge funds, returns of the financial markets, number of deaths in wars or casualties in terrorist attacks" (*Financial Times*, March 24, 2006). Disregard them at your peril (as the 2008 economic meltdown has illustrated so painfully).

This explains nicely the reason why people who value democracy in today's world need new techniques to maintain control by the public. Microsoft, the article says, controls most software sales, Google controls Internet traffic, interest rates jumped several thousand percent as recently as the 1990s, German currency inflation in the 1920s jumped millions of percent, one percent of the U.S. population earns ninety times the bottom 20 percent, and half the capitalization of the stock market (approximately ten thousand listed companies) is concentrated in fewer than a hundred corporations. "We live in a world primarily driven by random jumps, and tools designed for random walks address the wrong problem" (*Financial Times*, March 24, 2006).

Among the article's eight conclusions is the following: "When assessing the effectiveness of a given financial economic or social strategy, the observation window needs to be large enough to include substantial deviations, so one must base strategies on a long time frame" (*Financial Times*, March 24, 2006). This, I say, is why Hiroshima and Nagasaki must not be treated as ancient history. Deviations, yes—candidates for repetition, also yes.

The *Boston Globe* carried a piece by Janine R. Wedel that reviewed the 1990s-era scandal concerning Harvard University; its employee, economist Andrei Shleifer; and Shleifer's friendship with Lawrence Summers, later Clinton's secretary of the treasury, then president of Harvard, and now chair of President Obama's National Economic Council, but at the time of the controversy a Treasury Department official (Wedel 2006). The United States funded a Harvard-based consulting program to guide the Russian government in its economic privatization agenda. Ultimately Harvard and Shleifer settled charges of conspiracy to defraud the government that were brought by the Justice Department for $26.5 million and $2 million, respectively. Wedel reported:

> The endowment funds of both Harvard and Yale gained access to valuable investments through networks inhabited by Shleifer and/or his currency-trading wife. His investments in Russia, which he does not deny, included securities, equities, oil and aluminum companies, real estate, and mutual funds— many of the same areas in which he was being paid to provide impartial advice.
>
> Traditional accountability frameworks are no match for the ways in which today's diffused authority provides new opportunities for players to brandish influence, evade culpability, and gain deniability, while writing the new rules of the game. While Shleifer must pay a settlement and legal fees, it is

too late for the Russian people, who, instead of wise guidance, got corruption and a system wide open to looting. Until the United States devises better ways to track the networks and activities of these new players, it is destined to have an ever more untransparent and unaccountable system, with grave implications for democracy. (Wedel 2006, 1)

"Diffused authority" and the "implications for democracy" are the points to notice, for here is where our security system sits as well. Who is empowered to commit American troops, initiate preemptive war, mortgage the economy of future generations? At what point is democratic decision-making involved? How many Americans try to form a personal judgment about such matters and affect the outcome? If a large number did form independent judgments and worked to affect the outcome, what and where would they work? If they tried to achieve a global scope in their democratic participation, how would they do that?

A Deliberation Model

Americans need to craft democratic controls that work. They need to stop tolerating doomsday scenarios that remain elusive because they are statistically unlikely or because authority (read law and order, read enforced law, read war prevention) is diffuse.

The Center for Deliberative Democracy at Stanford University, headed by James S. Fishkin, created a public discussion format that has been tested around the world. In Texas and Louisiana discussions dealt with consumer willingness to pay more for utilities fueled by renewable energy. In Australia they dealt with proposed constitutional changes and relations between indigenous and other Australians. In New Haven they addressed regional economic policy; in Denmark, acceptance of the euro; in Great Britain, the monarchy and membership in the European Union; in Bulgaria, integration into civic life of the Roma (Gypsy) people; in China, public works; in Greece, a mayoralty election; in Northern Ireland, the relationship of Catholic and Protestant education systems.

The technique is to recruit three hundred to five hundred participants willing to devote a weekend to the announced issue. Before recruitment, sample polling of the participants ensures the presence of a range of citizens impacted by the issues to be explored. Participants are sent outlines of competing policy options along with arguments for and against each option. During the weekend, participants rotate through small-group discussions and plenary sessions where experts and policymakers answer questions. Questionnaires completed before and after the group discussions reveal that the deliberations result in marked shifts in opinion.

Professor Fishkin and Professor Bruce Ackerman of Yale University expanded the idea in *Deliberation Day*. They propose to pay every registered U.S. voter who will sign up $150 to participate in group deliberations for one of the two days of a national holiday that would be declared two weeks before each presidential election. During deliberation day, the key election issues would be deliberated upon in small- and large-group sessions as described above.

Keeping always in mind the great numbers of thinking, acting, fallible, loving, and hating people who put their shoulders to the wheel of social action, and their need for self reward as the generations turn over, not forgetting the inspiration, tolerance, and patience they must discover among themselves, let us consider how, one way or another, they have tried to shape their world over the generations, and then how we might shape ours.

While the pressures of [the Revolutionary] war lasted, the state assemblies generally concurred in what Congress asked of them. But even before the war ended, the defiance or noncompliance of individual states against congressional actions had become commonplace. (Morgan 1988, 265)

To create a national government resting on the whole people of the nation was perhaps the obvious solution, and since 1780 a constitutional convention had been the obvious way of achieving it. But the kind of government that could challenge and overcome the deficiencies of the state governments was not immediately apparent. . . .

Madison seized on Hume's insight. The trouble with the representative assemblies of the states was that the states were too small. In each of them groups with special interests were able to form popular majorities to carry out measures that were unfair to other groups. (Morgan 1988, 268–69)

When Madison and his colleagues at Philadelphia in 1787 invented an American people and gave them a government, it was with a view to overcoming the factions and the politicians in the state governments. (Morgan 1988, 305)

—from *Inventing the People* by Edmund S. Morgan

CHAPTER 13

Revisit the Foundations

To remold the civic world may seem an unrealistic assignment, but history often has seen people rise to necessity's demand for civic invention.

City, State, Security, and War

In *The City in History*, Lewis Mumford reviewed five thousand years of urban history and concluded that the city must become "an essential organ for expressing and actualizing the new human personality—that of 'One World Man'" (Mumford 1961, 573). Mumford posited such a development as the alternative to "the inertia of current civilization [which] still moves toward a worldwide nuclear catastrophe" (Mumford 1961, 573). On the one hand, "[e]ven a misinterpreted group of spots on a radar screen might trigger off a nuclear war that would blast our entire urban civilization out of existence and leave nothing behind to start over with." Yet, he says, "Our modern world culture, with its ever-deepening historic sources and its ever-widening contacts, is far richer in still unused potentialities, just because it is world-wide, than any other previous civilization" (Mumford 1961, 527–28).

Mumford calls war an "urban institution." Aggression first limited to raids, sallies for single victims, and religious sacrifices to promote fertility and crops "turned into the exhibition of the power of one community, under its wrathful god and priest-king, to control, subdue, or totally wipe out another community" (Mumford 1961, 42). Primitive magic, originally a childish dream, became an adult nightmare.

Redemption was close, says Mumford, when Athens invented democracy. This was a hundred-year project. In sixth-century BCE Greece, Solon was responsible for the disburdening ordinance, which reinfranchised debtors: "Many brought I back to their God-built birthplace who, justly or unjustly, had fled the creditors, lost to the sounds of Attic, wandering all over, and those who right here trembled in shame at their masters' whims, I set free" (Tejera 1993, 22). Judging that restoring rights destroyed by the oligarchy had recharged the civic, economic, and defensive health of the state, Victorino Tejera concludes, "Solon was not just the patrician grandfather of Athenian democracy but the founder of the vitality and participatory nature of Athenian common or public life" (Tejera 1993, 24).

Mumford describes Athens ultimately placing the "direct citizen responsibility and participation that had existed in village government" in the hands of an entire class of forty thousand citizens. While these constituted only one-seventh of the residents, this arrangement dispersed authority and separated political power from religious power. Lower offices were distributed by lot and rotated yearly (Mumford 1961, 155). The two-hundred-year republican experiment in Athens failed, says Mumford, because the Greeks never made a transition from direct democracy to representative government, and because they were seduced economically into huge public building projects financed by the spoils of war. Athenians became enamored of their city as an institution and made a god of it. They "lost hold of the greatest gift of divinity—that of transcending natural limitations, and pointing to goals beyond any immediate fulfill-ment" (Mumford 1961, 170).

In the meantime, though, while the democratic experiment was still succeeding, before "the synergy had turned partly into a concentration of [building] stone and part of it was dispersed in the wastage of war" (Mumford 1961, 168), the city and citi-zen reinforced one another's highest and best qualities. Along the same lines, Mumford says, "War, even when it is disguised by seemingly hardheaded economic demands, uniformly turns into a religious performance; nothing less than a wholesale rit-ual sacrifice" (Mumford 1961, 42).

For two-hundred-plus years, Rome also practiced limited democracy. In Rome's Augustan, imperial age, though, as Rich-ard Sennett says, Romans came to treat their public lives as a formal, impersonal obligation. Civic duties were performed without passion. Public life grew bloodless. Private energy and emotion gravitated to the mysticism of the Middle Eastern sects from which Christianity emerged, escaped the private realm of spiritualism, and came to dominate a new public order that assigned minimal value to civic creativity (Sennett 1977, 3).

Americans, Sennett thinks, approach the state with resigned acquiescence. Little pleasure is taken in the cosmopolis, the city, which Sennett dubs the world of strangers. As in Roman times, he suggests, participation in the *res publica* today is just going along, and the forums for this public life, like the city, are in a state of decay. Each person's self has become his princi-pal burden; to know oneself has become the end, instead of a means through which one knows the world.* Sennett goes on to say that we may understand that a politician's job is to draft

* In an article entitled, "Harvard's Crowded Course to Happiness," the *Boston Globe* (March 10, 2006) reported that Harvard College's most popu-lar course, attracting some five hundred students, called Practical Psyche, teaches meditation and breathing and asks students to ruminate, "What did I do right today?"

or execute legislation, but that work does not interest us until we perceive the play of personality in political struggle. A political leader running for office is spoken of as "credible" or "legitimate" in terms of what kind of man he is, rather than in terms of the actions or programs he espouses (Sennett 1977, 3, 4).

A writer whom Mumford praises for insight into urban history is Peter Kropotkin. Kropotkin, like Mumford, thought that people prefer peace when they can get it: "Quarrelsome rather than fierce, he prefers his cattle, the land, and his hut to soldiering" (Kropotkin 1970, 224). In the middle ages, civilization, centered in villages, achieved an era of tranquility; Kropotkin called villages "organisms bubbling with life" (Kropotkin 1970, 229). Some communities, once they grew into cities, formed alliances that transcended national boundaries with communities with which they had common interest. Kropotkin admired English, Dutch, and French port towns on each side of the English Channel, as well as Novgorod, and the Hansa communities in Germany and Scandinavia, for their supranational relationships.

The Hanseatic League achieved trade advantages for some seventy municipalities over a three-hundred-year period, reaching an apex in the mid-fourteenth century. Member cities were spread around the North Sea and the Baltic Sea as well as inland along the Rhine and other rivers. The league removed customs barriers between the members, acquired trade privileges with both states and nonmember cities, resisted the hegemonic ambitions of princes, and policed trade channels against piracy. Representatives met at Lübeck in an assembly called the Hansetag, where policies were adopted and disputes between member towns adjudicated.

When the state in the form of military chiefs, judges, and priests, whom Kropotkin termed the barbarians, seized villages and appropriated common lands, they subjugated the individual and "expected him to forget all his unions based on free agreement and free initiative. . . . They destroyed all ties between men" (Kropotkin 1970, 235). Elsewhere he continues, "The state is synonymous with war. Wars devastated Europe and managed to finish off the towns which the state had not yet directly destroyed" (Kropotkin 1970, 237).

History abounds with reasons to be wary of concentrating power into the hands of a few. The creators of the American form of government, to name just one example, had plenty to say on the subject.

Founding Debates in America

During the debates that preceded ratification of the U.S. Constitution, many feared that a federal government would overwhelm fealty to the individual states. In Federalist No. 46, James Madison responded, "A local spirit will infallibly prevail much more in the members of the Congress, than a national spirit will prevail in the Legislatures of the particular States." Still a sound observation, and most would agree that, to the extent that love of nation exceeds love of individual states, this is to the good. The point is that if our international and regional security federation did succeed in comanding affection, it would not be to the detriment of its member nations.

In Federalist No. 10, Madison asserts that in a larger republic it would prove more difficult for unworthy candidates to practice "vicious arts" and more difficult for a majority to invade individual rights. A larger sphere, he thought, demands and engenders more talent and dilutes nefarious schemes. While these chapters do not advocate a global republic, Madison's reasoning remains sound, to which might be added that corporate financial powers having become globalized, and having proved a fount of arms competition and of exploitation leading to conflict, global political machinery is needed as counterweight.

In Federalist No. 37 Madison notes the need for large states and small states to avoid the conflicts that their dissimilarities provoke, precisely a problem for nations in today's shrunken world. Federalism, moreover, would answer to dissimilarities beyond those of size. Madison observes:

> Nor could it have been the large and small States only which would marshal themselves in opposition to each other on various points. Other combinations, resulting from a difference of local position and policy, must have created additional difficulties. As every State may be divided into different districts, and its citizens into different classes, which give birth to contending interests and local jealousies; so the different parts of the United States are distinguished from each other, by a variety of circumstances, which produce a like effect on a larger scale. (*Federalist* 1961).

In *Originalism, Federalism, and the American Constitutional Enterprise*, Edward A. Purcell Jr. debunks the idea that the substitution of the Constitution for the Articles of Confederation amounted simply choosing a strong central government. The Constitution was criticized by anti-Federalists not just for augmenting central power but for hobbling power by overdividing and checking it. Power allocations favored not only three federal governmental branches, with the legislative branch further divided between two houses, but three levels of government—federal, state, and local. Anti-Federalist fears were grounded in uncertainties as to how the multiple division lines would play out (Purcell 2007, 28–29). The framers, however, intended sovereignty to reside not with the federal government but with citizens. The republican, or representative, form of government checked power by withholding the power to govern directly, rendering sovereignty "virtually impossible to locate" (Purcell 2007, 19). Purcell quotes Justice Joseph Story, speaking to the Suffolk County Bar in 1821: "Frame constitutions of government with what wisdom and foresight we may, they must be imperfect, and leave something to discretion, and much to public virtue" (Purcell 2007, 29).

To reassert a basic thesis, power (or sovereignty) always resides somewhere. If the public does not claim its share in realms that it can affect and—as Justice Story would say—use it virtuously, then the magnets of money, media, celebrity, ambition, and hatred proportionately expand their fields of attraction. Power is requisite to utilizing civic virtue.

Alexander Hamilton, in Federalist No. 22, says that the foundations of national government must be laid deeper than in "the mere sanction of delegated authority. The fabric of American empire ought to rest on a solid basis of the consent of the people. The streams of national power ought to flow immediately from that pure original fountain of all legitimate authority" (*Federalist* 1961). Similarly, in No. 46 Madison rebutted those who thought that, under the new Constitution, the federal and state governments would be continually at sword points:

> They must be told that the ultimate authority, wherever the derivative may be found, resides in the people alone; and that it will not depend merely on the comparative ambition or address of the different governments, whether either, or which of them, will be able to enlarge its sphere of jurisdiction at the expence of the other. Truth no less than decency requires, that the event in every case, should be supposed to depend on the sentiments and sanction of their common constituents. (*Federalist* 1961).

It will be objected that efforts to use municipal security conferences to influence national behavior and edge toward global democracy aspire to surmount complexities beyond the public's organizational capacity. Reflect, though, on Purcell's characterization of the tectonics that confronted our forefathers after ratification:

> Incorporating a diverse, unstable, and multiplying potpourri
> of institutions and interests, it was multifaceted and kaleido-
> scopic: tripartite on one side; fragmented and multitudinous
> on the other; and inherently volatile in the ways its innumer-
> able components and subcomponents linked their interests,
> checked their rivals, shifted their alliances, and justified their
> varied and countless demands in terms of the Constitution's
> doubly blurred lines of authority. (Purcell 2007, 49)

The words *national, federal,* and *sovereignty* do not appear in the Constitution (Purcell 2007, 28), and no mention is made of political parties or judicial review. Still, a federal system was assembled, and it worked.

In Federalist No. 27 Hamilton observed that, once familiar with the larger government, individuals would form an attach-ment to it, implying that they would effectively control it and reduce the occasion for armed conflict.

> Man is very much a creature of habit. A thing that rarely
> strikes his senses will generally have but little influence upon
> his mind. A government continually at a distance and out of
> sight, can hardly be expected to interest the sensations of the
> people. . . . The more it circulates through those channels and
> currents in which the passions of mankind naturally flow, the
> less will it require the aid of the violent and perilous expedi-
> ents of compulsions. (*Federalist* 1961)

Madison, in No. 14, tries to extinguish the bugaboo of uniqueness, surely a hurdle for our municipal congress: "Hear-ken not to the voice which petulantly tells you that the form of government recommended for your adoption is a novelty in the political world; that it has never yet had a place in the theories of the wildest projectors; that it rashly attempts what it is impossible to accomplish" (*Federalist* 1961).

To be sure, Madison goes on the extol the "kindred blood" of Americans and the fact that they recently had experienced the uniting force of the Revolution as factors that would simplify the task. Let us remember, though, that for all of the differences among peoples of the world, modern communication brings them together, and that they or their immediate forebears witnessed the carnage of the twentieth century. Hiroshima and Nagasaki taught a lesson unlike that any generation has experienced. Today's populations have more in common, and know they have more in common, than differences in lifestyles, dress, and language suggest. Give people a chance, I say, to collaborate on security over the heads of interest group configurations that freeze their national governments. Capacity for invention and cooperation will emerge and strengthen.

Democracy, wealth, superpower, communications technology, and the federal system give today's Americans an unprecedented range of civic tools. City, state, and nation are not mutually exclusive, but if one wants to discuss issues, contend with those in disagreement, unite with the like-minded, escape the constraints of nationalism's hypocrisies, and promote authentic democracy here and abroad, cities are the logical medium for our age.

To make a virtue of our supreme danger, we need not be as adventurous as Madison, Hamilton, and their colleagues, but civic invention may yet prove humanity's ace in the hole.

A global democracy capable of countering the anti-democratic tendencies of Jihad and McWorld cannot be borrowed from some particular nation's warehouse or copied from an abstract constitutional template. Citizenship, whether global or local, comes first.

These lessons would not be so hard for the complacent denizens of McWorld and the angry brothers of Jihad if the idea of civil society had retained its currency among those who call themselves democrats today. But battered by history and squeezed between two equally elephantine state and private market sectors, civil society has fairly vanished both as theory and as democratic practice. (Barber 1995, 279)

—from *Jihad* vs. *McWorld* by Benjamin R. Barber

Because democratic institutions do not renew themselves as effortlessly as flowering trees, they demand the ceaseless tinkering of people who possess both the courage and the honesty to admit their mistakes and accept responsibility for even their most inglorious acts. . . . Consider that Athens in the fifth century B.C. was as small as Dayton, Ohio, and then consider what would happen if, by removing the burden of cant and superstition, the United States could release the immense reserves of thought and energy in a population of 220 million people. (Lapham 1990, 371)

—from *Imperial Masquerade* by Lewis H. Lapham

CHAPTER 14

Ace in the Hole—
Civic Invention

The key to civic invention, grounded mostly in trial and error, is patience steeled with determination. Millions nurtured by and habituated to the war system, many of them fatalists who tolerate war as inevitable, must be coddled, stalled, outwitted, overcome, defeated, and occasionally even convinced. Translate the logic of law into practical politics, and global order advocates can prevail, provided that democratic restraints accompany the process.

So much travel, immigration, employment and educational exchange, and teaching and learning occur, so much good will gets exhibited that it is a marvel that war persists. Yet the profits, habits, history, and ideology of war are fused in our collective psyche. Hope for peace, dispersed and diluted among millions of hearts and minds, is not intuited as logical or natural. Irrationally, war seems logical; it is peace that must be invented. Its twin requisites—enforcement power and democratic control of that power—must be created.

Good will is endemic until it is defeated by injustice, real or imagined. People need to transform themselves from supplicants before governments molded by the war system—meaning all governments—to power wielders of a world system that enfolds security, the environment, and the regulation of economies and trade in an international system of enforced law. If good minds will apply themselves, all sorts of experiments wait to be tried.

Give Us Five Years

Grant, for discussion, that five years have passed since the first security conference of elected municipal representatives. Now a hundred municipalities attend the annual conference, or linked regional conferences. Their standing validated by elections, they have proposed to national governments a progressive, verifiable schedule of arms control.

The hundred cities and towns, enlarged by dozens every year, assign study groups and initiate monitoring committees to observe and comment on the progress, or deterioration, of their nations' efforts to resolve those conflicts. The elected municipal representatives report back to home populations. They command space in local media. Millions ponder as never before their stake in global affairs, and above all their security.

The conference agendas have expanded beyond the verification and enforcement of arms production, trading, and deployment. Alternative security guarantees, in the form of regional and international forces, are discussed. Municipal democracy begins to undercut such grounds for terrorism as national complicity in the surrender of natural resources to corporations, and the chartering of those corporations to ravage those resources for the benefit of profligate consumerism. Publicity exposes the diversion of wealth from indigenous people—for example, the Nigerian surrender of coastal oil extraction to Shell, Exxon, and other oil companies, and the Congolese surrender of copper, cobalt, and other mining interests. Norms, or rules, become regularized that ensure peace between ethnic and religious enclaves that history has left in risky proximity.

The annual conferences identify and publicize nuclear targeting. Targeted cities are mapped and their citizens apprised. Mutually targeted cities are paired, and their residents insist they be mutually detargeted. Even Indians and Pakistanis now have second thoughts about the jubilation when their governments first tested nuclear weapons.

There also has been a movement to detarget areas containing historical buildings, museums, religious centers, and universities. The process has enticed nations to announce reciprocal exceptions—exchanged immunities—supplemented by verification inspections. The inspections, in turn, make terrorist organizing more difficult. Organizing centers are exposed, as nations seem more like defenders than exploiters of cultures. Just as industries currently acknowledge global warming and participate in emissions trading across national boundaries, nations now trade immunity from WMD.

The security conferences attract philanthropic and taxpayer support. Conference staff members advance the work between conferences, publishing reports and commanding media attention. They make war prevention realistic and respectable. Peace becomes a pursuable goal, no longer squeezed from public discourse on grounds that such talk saps a nation's strength and encourages enemies.

Terrorist organizations are on the defensive because municipalities provide victims of religious intolerance, corporate exploitation, and human rights violations voices in corridors of power. Municipal delegations from terrorist-targeted cities visit terrorist home towns in Pakistan, Iran, and Afghanistan. National governments, discredited as a recourse against injustice, are succeeded by municipalities that listen and speak on a human level. Nonviolent modes of recourse against exploitation replace terrorist barbarism.

Grant all this, but still, how ever will the hugeness of the world, the vast numbers of people, the unwieldiness of large elected bodies, the diversity of languages and cultures, ever be accommodated in a mutual endeavor? How might such progress not break on the size and complexity of it all? Here are some experiments for our expanding congress of municipalities to undertake.

Build Cross-Border Election Districts

To achieve supranational representative bodies, large constituency districts will evolve, as will layered representative bodies—district assemblies electing some of their number to regional assemblies, which elect some of their number to global assemblies. However, direct elections to one or more world bodies are quite feasible. While initially centered in cities and towns, constituencies would expand to embrace all populations and some of the constituent districts would cross national boundaries. Possible ideas for constituency formation include these:

- Constituency representation might rotate. A geographic area could enjoy representation at the world level for five or ten years and then be unrepresented for five or ten years, or be shifted for a time from representation by direct election to representation as a component of a larger region or through representatives in regional assemblies.

- Some voting districts might be drawn with regard to identity of interests. People sharing a desert region, a watershed, an agricultural area, or neighboring urban areas would vote together some of the time on regional security policy, on advisory, or regulatory bodies. People exploited in a common way, or by common corporate interests, or deprived of common kinds of natural resources (e.g., Nigerian Ogonis and Canadian Inuits) might combine their legal and financial resources in a specialized parliament. Cultural groups separated by national boundaries might achieve common representation with respect to common security issues. If the Kurds in Iraq, Iran, and Turkey shared a representative, those three national governments might find themselves spared Kurdish separatist demands, the threat of Kurdish terrorism, and perhaps civil war.

Philip Bobbitt offers something similar: "This move to the primacy of persons as individuals and as members of self-chosen groups rather than only as nationals has several other implications for global governance. . . . [I]t ought to be possible for individuals to be citizens of more than one state and for their states to be members of more than one regional group" (Bobbitt 2008, 508).

Anti-Federalist Richard Henry Lee, writing as "Federal Farmer" to oppose ratifying the Constitution, argued that a sixty-five member House of Representatives never could represent "the interests, feelings, and opinions of three or four millions of people" (Weinstock 2001, 63). One reason that American democracy survived despite far larger constituencies than Federal Farmer imagined is that most constituents leave political concerns to others. Democracy serves activism; it responds to enunciated needs, and mediates between competing interests. Most people, politically passive, travel as passengers.

To focus initially on security will limit the range of issues. We are not proposing world government; we are exploring how to enhance security. The trick is to achieve a citizenry that agrees to disagree on a limited range of possible formulations of problems and solutions.

The founding municipalities will adopt election standards. Election supervisors will certify when a municipality has adopted acceptable rules and whether an election is valid. Municipal aspirations to join will get democracy's foot in the door of some of the authoritarian nations. National governments of all stripes will try to advance national agendas through their municipalities, and this will give municipalities common cause regardless of how their national politics are played.

American national and state elections are so flawed that they can hardly be cited as preferable to any proposal that would prohibit the gerrymander and invent ways to make issues rather than personalities, party label, and geography the deciding factors. In fact, global democratization, emboldened by the charge to avoid the mistakes of existing democracies, will prove healthy for national politics. Building up from cities and creating election districts based on interest rather than geography will trigger an overdue look at democracy's structure.

Employ Security Deposits to Guarantee International Law Compliance

Tens of thousands of commercial security transactions are entered into every day. Real estate, factory equipment, vehicles, securities, and cash are pledged to secure promises to do, perform, or refrain from myriad acts and obligations. This amply modeled device should be placed at the service of international order. As security for promises made, parties to an arms-control agreement could deposit assets with an international body—say, in the case of a major power, a hundred billion dollars. If international compliance inspection revealed prohibited weapons development, production, deployment, or sales, an international court would declare an appropriate forfeit. Money pledges could secure as well adherence to promises respecting human rights observance, environmental protection, and prohibitions on human or natural resource exploitation.

If an adjudicatory body were empowered to fine nations billions of dollars, imagine the progress that would occur on enforcement of the Nuclear Non-Proliferation Treaty. Absent means of enforcement, the vested interests of nuclear weaponry—financial and ideological—have prevented progress. For thirty-eight years, the black marketing of enriched uranium and pilfered weapons and components has continued while the security of hundreds of urban populations has shrunk. The monetary reward and punishment structure needs to undergo a complete turnaround.

Earnings on the security deposits would remain available to the nation-state depositors. So long as penalties were not imposed, deposits would constitute investments. For nonoffenders the cost would be minimal. Domestic public opinion would shift in a hurry against a government that wastes taxpayer resources by forfeiting pledges. In any event, for anyone whose values are in order, gambling in diplomacy with money instead of soldiers' lives would signal huge moral progress.

At least since John Maynard Keynes, economists have recommended the adoption of an international currency reserve, which Keynes called "bancor," and Joseph E. Stiglitz in *Making Globalization Work* calls "global greenbacks" (Stiglitz 2006). The idea is to replace the inherently unstable practice of borrowing, for purposes of national reserves, huge amounts of whatever nation's currency exhibits the most dependable value.

Trillions of dollars in currency serves a variety of purposes collateral to the principal purpose of providing a medium of exchange. A stable source of reserves, and security deposits that secure arms-control undertakings, might be pursued as companion objectives. If nations loaned currency to a global fund from which nations could borrow for reserves, and if repayment by the fund depended on adherence to global agreement, two birds might be killed with one stone.

Recruit Visitors

Consider the advantages that mobility holds for cohesion. Municipal engagement for security could recruit workers, students, emigrants, scholars, conference attendees, and tourists who cross borders to structure part of their experiences around building security. Municipalities might offer visitors and their own citizens who are planning trips incentives to register as participants in the security program. The incentive could include local transportation subsidies, free language and cultural classes, educational trips, and so forth, in return for which travelers communicate enthusiasm for electing delegates to the annual municipal security conference.

Create World Citizens

Establish a World Citizenship program that offers rewards as a stake in the peace system. In every nation people would learn that to be a World Citizen conferred travel, employment, educational, tax, and purchasing advantages without a surrender of existing citizenship. Qualification for World Citizenship might be earned in a variety of ways so that individuals could tailor plans to qualify in a manner consistent with their own lifestyle, agendas, and schedules. Credits toward qualification might include:

- Achieve command of two languages in addition to one's native language.

- Reside for a year in each of two countries.

- Host visitors from other nations.

- Pay a one percent tax surcharge to support global charities or peacekeeping costs.

- Be employed for two years by a global employer like the UN, World Health Organization, World Bank, or UNICEF.

- Earn a university degree in world citizenship, with required courses in, for example, history, language, comparative government, international law, and peace enforcement.

- Participate in programs like the municipal, regional, and global assemblies outlined in earlier chapters.

- Pass an examination.

Municipalities would accord prestige and advantage to their World Citizens. National governments might include native World Citizens in their cabinets, and perhaps, for limited purposes, nonnative World Citizens. World Citizenship would be a function of knowledge, understanding, and demonstrated freedom from antagonistic bias. It would be nonpartisan in the sense of requiring no commitment to a particular political, economic, social, or religious view. Each of us lives in a variety of societies—economic, religious, geographic, intellectual. World Citizenship would invite individuals sick of the war system to structure a personal identity geared to mutual acceptance of responsibility for universal security.

Former New Jersey Senator Bill Bradley, citing the citizenship conferred by our communities and nation, says, "[y]ou no longer can be a responsible member of a smaller community without being a world citizen, too. . . . Being a citizen of the world does not mean weakening our attachment to our personal communities, but rather strengthening our attachment to the rest of humanity" (Bradley 2007, 50).

World Cities
Cities might qualify as World Cities, earning qualification points by:

- Holding an electoral vote to accept World City designation and responsibility;

- Electing a local representative to the global or regional security assembly;

- Sponsoring citizen, employment, investment, and cultural exchanges;

- Adopting sister cities and exchanging students, faculties, employees, and tourists;

- Maintaining global centers—institutions that would host travelers and facilitate mutual understanding and cooperation.

National governments of World Cities would be challenged to accord distinction and prestige to their city participants.

Specialized cities are not unknown in history—for example, "free cities" that designated themselves free trade areas, and "open cities" that designated themselves as nondefensible and open to enemy occupation in time of war.

Over the eighty years from 1950 to 2030, the proportion of the world's population living in cities is expected to double from 30 percent to 60 percent (UN-HABITAT 2006, 5). Tokyo's population today is 35 million. Within ten years, Mumbai, Delhi, Mexico City, Sao Paulo, New York, Dhaka, Jakarta, and Lagos each will have a population exceeding 20 million (UN-HABITAT 2006, 6). More than 150 Chinese cities now exceed a million residents, while only nine U.S. cities are that large (*New York Times*, October 13, 2008).

However, a *Wall Street Journal* report on United States population trends predicts that with the projected growth by one-third in forty years (i.e., a hundred million more people), "that concentration of population is likely to result in megacities of 25 million or more as people head to them for jobs, demographers predict, raising new worries about the spread of infectious diseases and of terrorism in dense areas" (Kronholz 2006).

These populations exposed for mass slaughter cry for a proactive effort to reduce the causes of terrorism. Seaport and airport radiation detection can never be foolproof. Professor Stephen Graham of Durham University criticizes reliance on the "fortress city" approach:

> Such a "fortress city" approach to "homeland security," whilst lucrative to burgeoning military and security sectors, is a red herring because it is largely ineffective against determined attackers who can simply select the next unprotected, soft target out of the millions of options on offer in contemporary cities. Moreover, such an approach also risks undermining the interchange, openness, flow and density that sustain cities in the first place. . . .
>
> The challenge, rather, is to work at all scales of governance and conflict mediation to try and ensure that the grievances, injustices, extreme ideologies, and hatreds that fuel political violence against cities and urbanites are, as far as possible, ameliorated. This must be done to the extent that the murderous assaults on urban soft targets, by terrorists, insurgents, and state militaries alike, are prevented or are rendered politically or ideologically illegitimate.
>
> Such a challenge is daunting. This is especially so as urban research, policy, and activism have tended to neglect the urbanization of political violence thus far, leaving the subject to international relations specialists. But, in an increasingly urbanized world dominated by intensifying resource conflicts, global warming, proliferating refugee, water, and food crises— sometimes precipitated by aggressive nation states and transnational terrorist groups—the process fueling the urbanization of political violence seems set to accelerate further. . . . The time for a specifically urban treatment of geopolitics, which concentrates on how local urban sites and infrastructure are enrolled into global networks of political violence, is upon us. (UN-HABITAT 2006, 151)

Enforce Global Law

Military strategists understand that the United States cannot be
the world's policeman. Colonel Joseph R. Núñez, chair of the
Art of War Department at the U.S. Army War College's Strategic
Studies Institute, says,

> NATO is getting tired of having to serve as the proxy both for
> the United Nations and feeble regional organizations. . . . The
> sad truth is that there will be ever more failed states requiring
> long-term multinational intervention. . . . What are the other
> regions of the world prepared to do to handle the next likely
> conflagrations, be they in Sudan, Fiji, Congo, Somalia, Bolivia,
> North Korea, or Nepal? We must get much more creative
> about preserving stability at such fault lines. Too many inter-
> ventions, like the African Union's in Darfur, are done in an ad
> hoc and episodic manner, little wonder they usually fail. What
> we need are more permanent regional security and defense
> organizations, supported by major powers. . . never mind any
> high-minded values. While states may have legitimate con-
> cerns about things like sovereignty, the alternative to con-
> structive cooperation is the wildfire of anarchy. . . . The United
> States and its allies should work to create a minimum of six
> additional security and defense organizations patterned on
> NATO—one each for North America, South America, Africa,
> the Asia-Pacific region, South Asia, and the Middle East. . . .
> Each of these new alliances would have to be prepared to rap-
> idly deploy at least a brigade-level force—about 6,000 troops
> with ground, sea, and air capacities—anywhere in its sphere of
> influence. . . . Each of these new organizations would need at
> least one big power as a member. (Núñez 2007)

This is a proposal to explore world-scale law enforcement.
Núñez addresses only the military dimension, but couple what
he says with rules for progressive, verifiable arms control,

adjudicatory adjuncts, and cross-border democracy to impose controls, and progress toward authentic security would emerge. Núñez hints that the proposal holds implications beyond simply stopping wars once underway: "Of course all of these new alliances would need the blessing of the United Nations Secretary General Ban Ki-Moon, and their efforts would be coordinated through the organization's Department of Peacekeeping Operations" (Núñez 2007). Standing international armies answerable to the UN but free of the Security Council's veto power would of course have to be a component of enforced abolition of nuclear weapons. If military strategists like Núñez are starting to think this way, political strategists had better hurry to contribute the democratic accountability dimension. Moreover, if accountability is not addressed, such strategies risk global tyranny followed by global havoc.

Enlarge the Rule of Law by Adhering to Customary Law

If high school graduates were required to be as familiar with the manner of creating international law as they are with how Congress and the president create law in the United States, Americans would improve their capacity to influence issues of peace and war. A short curriculum section added to mandatory American history courses would empower Americans to exercise the civic virtue their presidents are always flattering them about.

Article 38 of the Statute of the International Court of Justice codifies a principle of international law that the Supreme Court of the United States recognized in the case of *The Paquete Habana* (175 U.S. 677, 1900). In 1898 American warships had captured two Cuban fishing boats during the Spanish-American War; the boats were condemned as prizes of war by a U.S. District Court and sold at auction. Proceeds were paid to the U.S. Treasury. On appeal, the Supreme Court awarded damages to the owners of the boats, stating that fishing craft on the high seas had been exempt from capture as prizes of war "by an ancient usage among civilized nations, beginning centuries ago, and gradually ripening into a rule of international law" (Janis 2003, 44–45).

Article 38 provides that, in addition to treaties, judicial decisions, and the "teachings of the most highly qualified publicists of the various nations," the International Court shall apply "international custom, as evidence of a general practice accepted as law; [and] the general principles of law recognized by civilized nations" in settling disputes.

This clause is of the utmost importance. In *The Prudent Peace: Law as Foreign Policy*, John A. Perkins points out that the rule offers every nation—especially a nation as influential as the United States—a powerful tool. A nation can choose to add its weight to creating a norm or custom, or it can choose to prevent a practice or policy from becoming a custom. Perkins points out that this country could announce that it will follow particular rules respecting, for example, nonintervention, self-determination, and rights of access to resources, urge other nations to follow suit, and so move toward strengthening the rule adhered to.

Perkins takes a further step, recommending that the United States issue a declaration that it will seek an adjudicated resolution of all disputes that cannot be resolved by negotiation and diplomacy, subject to the willingness of other necessary parties to adjudicate "according to principles of law, including those widely accepted principles not yet established as binding law that have the character of law and are appropriate for acceptance as law" (Perkins 1981, 149).

As Perkins deftly shows, international law offers Americans a potent instrument with which to forge security, provided they eschew the seducements of singularity and empire.

CHAPTER 15

Measure of the Electorate

Jane Goodall saw a chimpanzee poke a straw in a hole to extract ants, and the cry went out: "Humans are not the only tool users!" Why the jubilation—did Goodall demote us or promote our cousins? Maybe the discovery signals hope. If chimpanzees have a hidden talent, we might, too. We need it, heaven knows.

Human prospects attract two kinds of pessimism, largely unspoken but ubiquitous and civically enervating. One says too many are stupid (or, too few smart), the other that human personality is irrational, or perverse, or self-destructive, or so inescapably instinctive that experience does not instruct. Each kind of pessimism forestalls organizing a secure world.

If we think the human race cannot achieve peace, why search for political candidates who are optimistic about human prospects? Instead, frame security issues as how to win wars. The complexities of war seem to present a more acceptable challenge than the complexities of global governance. One deadly but prevalent idea has it that compromise, conciliation, and power-sharing display weakness and invite attack by enemies whose enmity, it must be assumed, is inevitable. Another is that to transfer peacekeeping power to the United Nations would make war more likely, either

because there can be no such thing as everyone's best interest or because no diverse group ever could act in everyone's
best interest. Also, that weapons superiority makes Americans safer than verified limitations, because armed strength
deters attack (while, incidentally, it induces compliance with
our policies).

However, policies that aim to intimidate, that plan for unilateral attack, that enforce ad hoc policy aims rather than create and enforce law, that reject enforced law as the arbiter in
favor of superior force, all provoke competition from hostile
minds, including those in nonstate groups. Implicit is the necessity for winners and losers. Worse yet is the mindset that substitutes good and evil for right and wrong and even for legal and
illegal, and claims to impose the will of a judgmental God and
then claims that God as one's own. Objective justice is thought
unobtainable, and barriers to organizing the world for peace are
imposed on grounds that

- Human nature is inherently warlike and untrustworthy.

- Other societies are too warlike, undemocratic, primitive,
  hostile to our friends, or strategically inimical to vital
  interests like oil.

- Collective peacekeeping is not feasible because it relies
  on undependable partners.

All of this is why champions are needed to insist that enforced
law could in fact be achieved that limits weapons and prohibits
both interstate war and civil war, because

- Humans are rational, and reasoned analysis shows that
  unilateralism based on superpower status is more risky
  than enforced universal law, to which the United States
  must submit if others are to submit.

- Collective policing in which all nations participate is bound to be more effective than unilateral policing, assuming reliable and accountable command and control.

The more successful people are at persuading the rest of the world that they are irresistible and impregnable, the more readily they invite surreptitious attack. Fanatics with WMD and nothing to lose will prove a match for urban technocracies with everything to lose. If winning wars ever was the best route to security, that time is past. To the degree that these contrasting views reflect differences in education and upbringing, we ought to train more optimists. Whether training or personality is responsible, there is no solution short of placing different types of people in charge. Surely the 2008 elections will prove to have been a step in the right direction, but the ups and downs of sixty-five years prove the dangers of relying solely on any national government.

Human Nature Meets Civic Aspiration

One difficulty is that the military-minded gravitate to power. Peace-minded activists, as I have observed them, tend to not be power-oriented, although as a result of choice and practice, not capacity. Many such people are cynical about the misuses of politics and habituated to despise personal possession of power, yet remain hungry to influence events, as the 2008 elections showed. They must persevere in using their wits to overcome the gerrymandered, wealth-dependent distortions of America's political system and to find and use the power that is available.

The evolution of the human race is interesting to speculate about, but no one worries about where it will lead. Several generations of scientists and historians cannot measure so slow a process. It is difficult to guess what characteristics might help or hurt our distant descendants. As evolution cannot be charted ahead of time, advocates of preventing war have lacked a response to the widespread view that we shall always have war because it is part of "human nature." Anti-war advocates have failed to counter the idea that only evolution into a kinder, gentler race could prevent war. They have failed to insist that we concentrate on the better side of human nature and promote leaders to champion that side in deed as well as rhetoric.

Nuclear weapons make resignation in the face of disagreement about what can be done with human nature unacceptable. Never mind the immorality of not stopping war; the fate of humanity looms in the form of nuclear Armageddon. That is what the Iraq War was about, according to the Bush administration, however oil, politics, and poor judgment may have contributed. The rationalization was WMD, and that excuse or reason for America's preemptive attack has made Iran and North Korea, and will make other nations, flash points of doom.

Even those who despair at some of the rotten tendencies of the human makeup may find a measure of solace in contructive activity: if they are worried or if they have more confidence in human inventive and organizational powers than in the vagaries of imperceptible evolution, it is time to create a new arena for inventive political action.

David Barash, a professor of psychology at the University of Washington, Seattle, concludes that controlling our "new-found capacity to destroy the earth" is quite within our ability, for "[a] primate that can learn to control its bowels can do most anything" (Barash 2003, 44). Barash explains that humans, who evolved from tree dwellers that could eliminate without fouling their habitat require years to toilet train, while dogs and cats, whose ancestors were den dwellers, can be housebroken in a few days.

Anthropologist Margaret Mead called war a cultural invention, and advised:

> If we despair over the way in which war seems such an
> ingrained habit of most of the human race, we can take com-
> fort from the fact that a poor invention will usually give place
> to a better invention.
>
> For this, two conditions, at least, are necessary. The peo-
> ple must recognize the defects of the old invention, and some-
> one must make a new one. . . . A form of behavior becomes out
> of date only when something else takes its place and, in order
> to invent forms of behavior, which will make war obsolete, it
> is a first requirement to believe that an invention is possible.
> (Mead 2003, 104–105)

During World War I, Columbia University English professor
John Erskine gave a Phi Beta Kappa address at Amherst College. Erskine's thesis was that the British and American value
systems, derived from warlike progenitors who lived in German
forests, as reflected in English literature, preferred character to
intelligence. This contrasted, he said, with the views of those
whose values derived from the Greeks.

> We make a moral issue of an economic or social question,
> because it seems ignoble to admit it is simply a question for
> intelligence. . . . We applaud those leaders who warm to their
> work—who, when they cannot open a door, threaten to kick
> it in. In the philosopher's words, we curse the obstacles of life
> as though they were devils. But they are not devils. They are
> obstacles. (Erskine 1916, 25–26)

In law, Erskine observed, the exercise of human intelligence found a "better persuasion to honesty and enterprise"
than hanging thieves and flogging schoolboys (Erskine 1916,
25–26). In religion, human intelligence sought a surer route to
understanding God's will than animal sacrifices and mysteries.
Erskine predicted that his Phi Beta Kappa audience would be in

the thick of the fight "between this rising host that follow intelligence, and the old camp that put their trust in a stout heart, a firm will, and a strong hand" (Erskine 1916, 28).

The Amherst Phi Beta Kappas and other scholars shirked the battle, though, or lost it, considering what has transpired. Even if a few of those scholars heeded Erskine, the struggle to impose reason on public policy probably will consume more than the ninety-three years that have elapsed since Erskine's speech. The question for our more threatened generation is whether doomsday weapons will make more people try harder.

One weeps at the results of a survey conducted in thirty-two European nations plus the United States and Japan, asking whether humans developed from earlier animal species. Only the citizens of Turkey gave more negative responses than Americans did (*New York Times*, August, 15, 2006). Or at a report that in a mosque in Queens, New York, a class of boys aged seven to fourteen spends all day until 5:00 p.m., year round, memorizing the Koran (*New York Times*, August, 15, 2006). Education reform and school standards hold an answer to the dumbing down that these examples and a thousand more represent, but surer reliance would be found if those aware of looming holocaust and smart enough to do something about it determined to acquire the power to do something.

Greed bloated by access to national power motivates economic and political chauvinists to manipulate the hopes, fears, and votes of the ignorant, biased, irrational, and undereducated. To the degree that more power gets conferred on them due to superior numbers, they achieve more control than the educated, rational, responsible, and clear-headed. This might be said to double or triple the civic obligations of reflective, knowledgeable Americans, who must make up for perils their capable but neglectful compatriots aid and abet. Thinking ones are morally obliged to think harder and longer, vote more objectively, and participate more, not just because of their greater capacity to be useful, not because their nation's power multiplies their possible usefulness, but also to compensate for the power enhancement that manipulated, irresponsible citizens confer on private interests.

Surveys reveal that, despite more years spent in school, the vast majority of Americans know almost nothing about how their vaunted democracy works. Two in ten know there are one hundred U.S. senators. Four in ten can name the three branches of government. Rick Shenkman attributes the ignorance to television's replacement of newspapers as the primary news source (Shenkman 2008). Whatever the reason, it means that our cross-border rescue effort had better get busy.

Nearly fifty years ago John W. Gardner, in his passionate *Excellence*, called on Americans to raise their intellectual and civic standards and goals: "We should be painting a vastly greater mural on a vastly more spacious wall" (Gardner 1961, 142). Because the great problems are so complex, he said, the full extent of individual responsibility is not self-evident. However, "[f]ree men must set their own goals" (Gardner 1961, 161). Gardner, founder of Common Cause, emphasized the breadth and depth of citizen capacity throughout the society to improve and to contribute: "The tens and hundreds of thousands of citizens who have achieved positions of eminence and influence in our national life must live with a powerful sense of their obligation to the community and to the nation. They are our dispersed leadership" (Gardner 1961, 125). I would expand the call to include the few million who are not eminent, who see the doom, who must obtain the power, who must change the nation's course.

Leaders of national prominence could do so much to raise civic aspiration. A president should spend less time trying to persuade people to support particular policies and trust them to choose the best policies by raising their knowledge level. As an example, consider the unprecedented step of a president's making the kind of speech set forth in Appendix D.

Reactions to my line of argument rest on one's assessment of the human psyche and intelligence. Those who think few are intelligent, who equate shallow thinking with stupidity, will have little patience with strategies to enhance the products of democracy. However patriotic they fancy themselves, they are an easy mark for authoritarian approaches to policy issues. Those who think average intelligence is high but is of little use without education will be moderately intrigued by the suggestion that those with better and or less biased minds should work harder for public goals. Those who believe that no amount of wisdom or education can prevent the worst excesses on the grounds, for example, that humans are essentially irrational or selfishly motivated, or instinctively warlike, effectively give up on democracy, become fatalists, and must be counted as part of the problem and outvoted.

For those who do labor for the commonweal, democracy requires working with what you have. Resources for sound public judgment are disparate and impermanent. Dispassionate, informed people who will take responsibility and express themselves always are in short supply. Some cohesive, responsible core must subject events to analysis and the tests of history, intelligence, and practicality, must resist demagoguery and forsake self aggrandizement. Such a self-selected but infinitely expandable leadership will win elections often enough against those who assume the world is too large for orderly governance, that global governance could only end in tyranny or disaster for Americans in the form of economic leveling. But they will be resisted by those who think that human nature instinctively drives nations to war, even that periodic war is the inevitable, ultimate means to settle some conflicts or cull populations. More than resisted, they will be opposed heart and soul, because they challenge beliefs and advocate change.

To be optimistic, to believe that intellectual achievement will be valued in civic life and that democracy itself will survive, you have to believe that the intelligence of the average citizen is higher than most will allow, that more can learn and reason at a level commensurate with the problems to be solved. You have to believe, too, that intelligence appears in many forms. Optimism holds that political participation educates and sharpens, and that the quality of politics and government is sustained as well by enthusiasm, taste, and style. Altruism and civic pride nurture democracy quite as much as intelligence. You also have to believe in collective intelligence, one dimension of which is that succeeding generations can profit by previous mistakes.

America's early civic strength lay perhaps in the local character of people's interests, while its weakness stemmed from a relatively low level of education. Today the advantages gained through prolonged schooling are diluted by a thousand diversions. More are trained to reason and provided lessons of history, but proportionately fewer dedicate those resources to the public's business because events seem too remote to influence, and their capacities are diverted by the struggle for private rewards.

Even assuming that most people study and think before they vote (which they don't), elections are but one of democracy's essentials. Candidates must be chosen, campaigns paid for, information disseminated, debate achieved, workers recruited. Even thoughtful voting is meaningless without contested elections and real candidates as distinguished from figureheads and surrogates. So long as too few try to control city halls and state houses, and rigged electoral districts deny us contested elections, elections will neither express the will of the people nor produce first-rate leaders.

Democratic authenticity begins with citizens who obtain real power and think of themselves as power holders. That means having a degree of personal influence and control, shared with others but not to the point of insignificance, over some segment of society's wealth, education, laws, and the interplay between political power centers.

No one truly is a democratic citizen who cannot person-ally reach and influence, together with others, those who deter-mine how taxes are raised and spent; the content and teaching of school curricula; local government expressions about the policies of higher government; the legislating, adjudicating, and enforcement of laws; and the content and character of news reporting and commentary.

Enough have to share the power to influence holders of greater power to keep power fluid and dispersed. Democracy cannot long exist with an overconcentration of power. As politi-cal activism is the means to disperse power, a great many activ-ists are needed. So long as entry into the ranks of activists is open while nonactivists, by force of numbers, retain the ballot box veto power that is integral to democracy, a majority of citi-zens need not be active. Many more are needed, though, than are active today. Nonactivists, including those whose activism is limited to supplication through marching, protests, and resolu-tion-oriented conclaves, are not fully democratic citizens. They are onlookers, even as their majority veto serves, sometimes blindly, to check and balance.

The catchphrases "think globally, act locally" and "if you're not part of the solution, you're part of the problem" have not been construed as precepts for obtaining personal political power. As undeterrable terrorists prepare to murder Americans en masse, we the intended victims, ironically the superpower decision makers as well, await a cue. Civic attention, which long ago shifted from town to nation at the expense of personal involvement, now must confront the global. To do this requires more personal involvement, not less. The route to action leads back through the towns and cities. For anyone who decides to be proactive on behalf of stable, nurturing government, and agrees that it depends upon a deliberative, judgmental, experi-mental public, the municipality is the place to start.

Were we more open to self-analysis and self-criticism, Americans might accept greater personal responsibility for their civic performance. What inhibits us is that self-analysis produces a sense of not measuring up. The awareness of letting one's nation down prompts many of us to hide civic shortcomings under garish patriotism, and denigrate civic-minded neighbors as busybodies.

The test of our system is upon us. A rational response to nuclear terrorism would link the cause and effect of weapons, enriched uranium and its theft, war and proliferation, exploitation and hatred. Americans would ask, what are we doing wrong, what am I doing wrong? Civic self-assessment starts with evaluating our performance as an electorate. Do enough capable people join the effort to make up for those who vote in total ignorance? Do those who want to play an active role succeed in doing it? Do enough assume leadership roles without needing to feel it makes them more worthy? Do schools instill the sense of obligation? Do enough participate to prevent manipulation by the self-interested? Do Americans determine their own public policies? Does a promising electoral result, as in 2008, prompt too many to sit on their hands for the next four years?

We do not evaluate our public life very well. The best citizens, from the polity's viewpoint, are determined to stay objective, to vote on issues and not personalities. But objectivity also constrains them from passing the necessary civic judgment on fellow citizens. And those fellow citizens who try least to understand and vote on issues are the last to exercise self-criticism. They can only celebrate being Americans.

A public conscious of its commonalty only at the national level fails to communicate on the basis of the familiar, which is their segmented but associated communities. Instincts for expression are exhausted by preoccupation with trivia. People are satiated with snatches of a vast universe delivered like the music of the spheres by marketers, entertainers, politicians, and preachers, as well as boxes and discs and chips of canned and programmed noise and images. The ubiquity of sensations stifles the mind.

In his book *Democracy and Tradition*, Jeffrey Stout, citing Walt Whitman, observes that "we are not self-evidently fit to perform the tasks that our circumstances demand of us if we want to live democratically" (Stout 2004, 21). Stout identifies two kinds of thinking that give short shrift to civic character as a prerequisite to authentic democracy. The first is exhibited by "those who worship the people as a race or a nation, thus placing our character beyond question" (Stout 2004, 22). The second is discerned among "those who believe that our political and economic systems are structurally immune from whatever faults the people might have" (Stout 2004, 22).

Neither self-worshipers nor system-worshipers are likely to generate a response to the cataclysmic danger. Democracy's virtue is its capacity to magnify abilities and multiply virtues. To take personal responsibility for capitalizing on this virtue is the test of civic character. Better vehicles of personal involvement need to be invented, and attention needs to be paid to universal ahead of group problems. The civil rights, feminist, and gay rights movements were timely and necessary, and like all the battles against discrimination, hardly complete. However, the progress of groups is sufficient, and the common peril of all groups so great, that group strivers need to move beyond victimhood to imbue the whole society with their passion and strength.

One must not agonize over the disparity between the controlling powers of the few and the reasoning power of the masses. The public dialogue that these chapters advocate among municipal residents and between municipalities would expose, order, and harvest mass intelligence. If I believe that persuasion does not work because most are too dense to reason things, or because a different sort of person than I am will inevitably be in control, I may limit my exertions for the commonweal. We need to be less conclusive in our personality dissections and place more reliance on one another.

Thousands—not millions, just thousands—could nudge the nation to move, in time, from a war-predicated security policy to a security policy based on enforced law. Those thousands, say a hundred thousand, would run for the public offices that are accessible, or help others to run for those offices. City, town, and state governments are composed of tens of thousands of such offices, and they all command power. Once enough cities and towns begin to advocate, in common with cities and towns of other nations, for international institutions capable of forming and enforcing universal security law, nations must follow.

A secure world must be invented piecemeal, in multiple nations. It cannot be imagined or implemented as a unitary, preconceived plan or program. National leaders will not invent it. The context of their careers is too short-term. Even if a national government announced a brilliant, practical security plan, the public, especially the publics of other nations, would reject it because of its necessarily radical nature, and because it would entail sacrifices.

As the necessary global steps have not been and cannot be developed as top-down foreign policy, they must be invented at the bottom of the political hierarchy, regardless of what the Constitution says about the president being in charge of foreign policy. Even if a wise president and State Department create a plan for the nation's participation in a secure global arrangement, it will be opposed by the financial and ideological interests that depend on the war system unless a good deal of public discussion already has occurred. If enough Americans are not engaged in the control of their city halls and state houses, the quadrennial voting for president is not going to prevent Armageddon.

More citizens might be persuaded to participate in politics and government if they understood the degree to which local power can translate into global power. Most obviously, this occurs through party apparatus. A vigorous local party influences power holders through the selection of candidates and party platforms, the exercise of influence over office holders who depend on it for election and reelection help, the organization and informing of adherents, and the creation of pressure groups. Less readily appreciated is the ability to reach the public through local media. Add to this list the ability to motivate local governments to take positions on national political issues and the ability to communicate with counterpart populations in other states and countries, and you have a model for the security congress movement.

An awareness of how the idea of citizenship has evolved is useful in considering how to recast our own roles as citizens. Charlotte C. Wells describes shifts in how citizenship has been viewed in France over the course of three hundred years. That the modern view more closely resembles the sixteenth-century view than that of the late eighteenth-century revolutionary period argues against a passive acceptance of what evolution brings. Back when efforts began to coalesce fragmented duchies into a French nation, arguments were sought for the existence of a national citizenship. The idea was advanced that the state was one large city. One thrust of this conclusion, Wells notes, was that citizens should hold one another in high regard. Another was that if citizens had a common duty, it ran to the state: "Citizens were bound together by ties of neighborliness and participated in each other's grief and sufferings. . . . The metaphor of the state as a city thus gave rise to a vision of the moral community of all citizens" (Wells 1995, 89–90).

The mutual tolerance of Protestants and Catholics that this concept promoted, though, was succeeded by persecution of the Protestant Huguenots and religious wars: "The rising sun of absolutism led inevitably to the eclipse of the autonomous citizen as an actor on the political stage" (Wells 1995, 96). "Under the absolutist citizenship theory, the contract bound the individual and the prince, not the individual and the commonwealth," Wells says (Wells 1995, 112).What survived, as "a subterranean rivulet of citizenship theory, flowed beneath the soil of absolutism" (Wells 1995, 120). The citizen acquired rights by choosing to obey the monarch's laws.

Revolutionary theory located citizenship in community membership rather than by relation to the monarch. In common with Italian Renaissance theorists, citizens were subjects vis-à-vis the sovereign, but citizens when they exercised legal rights (Wells 1995, 133). With the revolution came the right to vote, but rights common to all by virtue of natural law (that is, civil rights) were disregarded (Wells 1995, 141). In its emphasis on the voting franchise, the 1791 French constitution restricted citizenship in a new way, by making "true citizens only of those who met its established franchise standards of age, gender, and property ownership." Others were passive rather than active citizens (Wells 1995, 142). As the Terror gathered force, there was proclaimed to be the "uncitizen," persons who made themselves foreign by not adhering to revolutionary ideals (Wells 1995, 143). After the revolution, the Code Civile returned the state to the earlier emphasis on civil rather than political rights.

The Point of Democracy

The right to vote, sacred even to Americans who don't vote, surely is an exaggerated blessing in the land of the gerrymander, the million-dollar TV ad, and the absence of political dialogue. The point of democracy is to achieve a reasoned allocation of power. If you are voting blindly or voting with no chance of being on the winning side, you are not engaging in democracy. If outcomes are determined by money, manipulation, and lies, they do not constitute democracy. Mere trappings are a complacency-inducing opiate. By the same token, if it takes an unnecessary war paired with chaos in the economy to elect a promising newcomer like Barack Obama, the best that can be said is that American democracy accommodates rescue.

Some who might agree grasp at the straw of Internet organization. Rapid communication facilitates organizing, but it reaches only the like-minded and allocates no power. Moreover, the Internet is covert. Not secret, to be sure, as it is open to all to join or observe, but covert because not pursued in the open. Democracy requires openness. Internet participation is just a new way for the like-minded to congregate. Blind armies marching and countermarching cannot maintain democracy, because the self-interested and the ideologues will out-organize them. American democracy is marred by fragmented citizen engagement on the one hand and fractious groupings on the other. MoveOn's 2008 performance revealed the Internet's capacity to coordinate the likeminded. It was not a facilitator of dialogue among all Americans.

Minimalist democracy is a veto arrangement by which voters are empowered to prevent the worst excesses of rulers by throwing the rascals out when corruption is revealed, or when they violate too many freedoms or pursue blatantly discredited policies. Where apathy, cynicism, and incompetence reign, this is the best one can hope for. Given an informed, interested electorate, on the other hand, a commonweal may emerge that can be evaluated by the soundness of public judgments, and whose stability and promotion of the better human attributes is almost bound to exceed that of the minimalist version.

In a fully realized democracy, the public would focus on policy choices that emerge from legislatures, bureaucracies, interest groups, and scholars, and would pass judgments on those choices. Making such judgments, however, pairs good minds with bad. Public-spirited citizens are yoked with the biased, selfish, and foolish. If thoughtful folk monopolize the dialogue, shallow ones, who must not be excluded, lash out. If the thoughtless dominate, able ones grow bored or disillusioned. All the while, greedy and messianic elements tear at the process.

Benjamin Barber writes:

> The idea of service to country or obligations to the institutions by which rights and liberty are maintained has fairly vanished. "We The People" have severed our connections with "It" the state or "They" the bureaucrats and politicians who run it. If we posit a problem of governance, it is always framed in the language of leadership: why are there no great leaders anymore? . . . [S]ervice has lost much of its political potency precisely because citizenship has lost its currency. It is a notion so thin and wan nowadays that it means little more than voting, when it means anything at all. Democratic politics has become something we watch rather than something we do. (Barber 1998, 187–88)

Barber notes the correlation of declining enthusiasm for citizen responsibilities with the spread of personal liberty and the voting franchise. He calls for institutional efforts to regain something of the ardor for public service that attended ancient Athens, when only a small fraction of the population enjoyed full governmental participatory rights. In his earlier book *Strong Democracy*, Barber explores the potential of a national system of neighborhood assemblies, universal citizen service, and national referenda and initiatives.

The need for stronger democracy and some of the tools necessary to accomplish it have long been evident. So has a sluggish, even peevish, resistance. Consider one of *Esquire* magazine columnist Chuck Klosterman's "America" columns: he concludes that nothing can be done about our democracy deficit even if a couple of hypothesized nightmares came true (Klosterman 2007). Suppose, he says, that after Hurricane Katrina the federal government did not only too little, but nothing at all. Or suppose that we learned that the government actually perpetrated 9/11, just as conspiracy theorists charge. Klosterman says that even if everyone agreed that these nightmares were reality, nothing could be done to correct matters:

> Security has a way of making philosophy irrelevant. . . . [T]
> here's still something ominous about the reality of our sanctu-
> ary. It seems weird that *this is the* country and there's nothing
> we can do about it, beyond participating in the system that's
> already in place. It would not matter what the government
> did or to whom they did it—nobody knows how to change
> things in any meaningful way, and the only people who'd try
> are dangerous and insane. We have reached a point where the
> reinvention of America is impossible, even if that were what
> we wanted. Even if that were what *everybody* wanted. (Klos-
> terman 2007 [Emphasis in original])

Those who are worried enough about security to try to disprove Klosterman have one and only one ready source of power to change things, and that is their municipal government.

The first time I ran for Cambridge School Committee, an experienced political manager offered advice. Many whose help you ask for, he said, who you think will say yes because they are friends or relatives, will turn you down or never lift a finger. Don't be angry or hurt; they are not politically oriented. Their disinterest will be more than compensated for by people you never knew who will emerge from nowhere and devote long hours to your cause. You won't know how to thank them, but never mind, they are doing what they love and value. Across thirteen times on the ballot and work on county, state, and nation campaigns, I found his analysis to be absolutely true.

Democracy rests on the self-selection by a minority as freedom's workhorses. Think of them as nosey, minding everyone's business. Think of them as maternal, nurturing their fellow citizens and an idea called freedom. Think of them as sentimental, revering a theory of government, or showing faith in an ideal.

They specialize among themselves, often to the point where they can't see what their efforts on behalf of the environment, education, health, peace, and so forth have in common. They come and leave the public table depending on family commitments, emotional strength, and occupational demands.

Now, I say, they need to self-identify, because they are the last, best hope. They need to identify themselves to one another because the armies of the ignorant and neglectful, measured by the threat we face, have never been larger.

"Some doubt that the problem of WMD terrorism can ever be solved. But if there is real, verified progress in disarmament, the ability to eliminate this threat will grow exponentially. It will be much easier to encourage governments to tighten relevant controls if a basic, global taboo exists on the very possession of certain types of weapons. As we progressively eliminate the world's deadliest weapons and the components, we will make it harder to execute WMD terrorist attacks."

—Ban Ki-moon, Secretary General of the United Nations (Schneidmiller 2008)

CHAPTER 16

Final Thoughts

For a prospective reader who might have turned to the end of the book, as I often do, to see whether the conclusion argues for reading the preceding chapters, let me say that this book is not about pacifism. National armies will remain necessary but can be scaled down as global and regional security resources—military, administrative, and judicial—scale up. The prerequisite for that scaling up, however, is democratic accountability exercised across national borders. Rather than trying to describe a model of such a world, these chapters have suggested steps by which concerned individuals might produce it.

I have offered eight arguments. Their exposition has not always been tidy, so I summarize them here, and offer a few thoughts toward making the arguments cohesive.

First, the perils of nuclear proliferation and terrorist possession of WMD mandate new approaches to security. They dictate finding a surer means than presidential voting through which Americans might influence security policy. Habit and tradition, the profitability of the war system, and the absence (usually) of anyone high in the power structure able—whether from conviction or political reality—to imagine a foreign policy not based on national military strength all cry for some of us to start innovating.

Second, WMD-age security must exist everywhere or nowhere, so the power to build an alternative security system must be sought in many nations, requiring outreach agencies more numerous and people-based than the world's state departments and war departments.

Third, because power, for anyone not immensely wealthy and able to manipulate mass communication, is achievable only through politics, and effectiveness in national politics and, to only a slightly lesser extent, state politics is foreclosed by money, media domination, and the gerrymander, municipal politics alone remains the attainable power source for intended victim populations. Cities and towns must serve as last-ditch agent for the building of security.

Fourth, some number of individuals, substantial but far less than a majority, must come to these conclusions independently and intellectually. This requirement is distinct from public opinion molding, which has reference to mass opinion and majority opinion. It is distinct as well from grassroots action, which suggests large numbers each doing a little. A viable future calls for many more individuals who will contend with fellow citizens intellectually and then politically.

Fifth, the civic quality of the electorate, or at least a critical segment of it, can no longer be left to chance. Some conscious act of creation or awakening must discover enough capable and engaged citizens to steer this nation, upon which the fate of the world may depend. Where and how we exercise our intellects and other abilities is as subject to fads as hair styles, though a longer period may be required to recognize the patterns. Today creativity is in for technology, science, business, art, and religion; it is out for humanitarianism, law, and peace. If I want to invent something that does not flash, ping, zap, rake in dollars, look pretty, or incite tears, I will be told not to waste my time—human nature is too aggressive, and too few of us are smart enough. The advice will be similar if I want to invent new routes to a secure world: wait for some great leader, or wait until some revealed and universal truth or compelling necessity commands adherence. This attitude relieves most of us, who are not engineers, entrepreneurs, artists, preachers, or supporting cast members like lawyers and doctors, from doing much thinking. For most Americans, life is clock-punching interspersed with sports, once-a-week piety, and occasional peace marches. Such resignation also relieves those who do think from thinking outside of their niches. Almost everyone is capable of effective civic work, and a vastly greater number must rise to the occasion of our security crisis. This plea, above all, is anti-elitist because it urges us to stop leaving control to big money, big business, big media, celebrities, professors, weapons inventors, and zealots.

Sixth, a precondition of all of the above is the need to create forums for discussion, amazingly lacking in our vaunted democracy. Again, this need leads back to cities and towns.

Seventh, to invent an effective political vehicle and commit to a development period long enough to achieve a stable world, and to engage cities and towns worldwide, we must ask how to engage fellow designated victims of the doomsday lockstep in democratic elections, including in some cases cross-border elections, to international bodies.

Eighth, the resulting democratic accountability will begin to make it safe and therefore feasible to confer the power to enforce law on international and regional institutions to prohibit creation, possession, and trade in WMD and to prevent war.

These eight efforts must work together, and citizens must be persuaded to participate by more than one of the eight themes at a time. While Chapter 5 identified a convenient, practical point of commencement and Chapter 14 offered some specific new departures, one cannot guess what ultimate configuration of politics and law will prove workable. I have not wasted time proposing constitutions. Neither have I asked the reader to suspend skepticism or abandon realism. The appeal has been to the reality that a credible impetus to crush the nation-based war system must flow from a power source greater than any incumbent government or any nongovernmental body can muster—the ballot box. Anyone who accuses a sympathetic reader of gullibility, utopianism, or idealism should be challenged as to his or her experience with both practical politics and the pursuit of power. This book's subtitle might indeed be Practical Politics and the Pursuit of Power.

As experimentation is central to the enterprise, I make no claim to invent full-blown institutions, strategies, or dependable action plans, and I discourage others from claiming that they can do so. The aim is to suggest a process that, over the course of say fifty years, might achieve a secure world. If fifty years seems like a long time, reflect on the peril occasioned by failing over the course of sixty-five years to control the atom, and the instant advantages that will attend civic invention.

I have not recommended anything that Congress, or the president, or "people" should do. Rather, I insist that some number of individuals must select themselves to act through the only segment of government within civic reach. Not what they should do to save their souls or find salvation. Not what their moral obligations might be. Rather, what is open, available, and waiting for free individuals to do—people who are free of legal impediment, free to empower themselves, free to persuade fellow citizens, free to win elections. Americans as they were expected to be two hundred years after their nation's founding, after two hundred years of education and prosperity—informed, active, responsible.

Epilogue

A young man in a sports jacket and open-collared shirt leaves his briefcase in the checkroom and sits at the bar in Louisville's Seelbach Hotel. He orders a designer bourbon from Seelbach's forty choices, looks in the mirror, lifts his glass in a toast—to hell, or Allah, or bin Laden, or the virgins he is going to ravish in the never-never land of terrorist dreams. In his briefcase is a nuclear bomb, and at 1:00 p.m. on a bright spring day, a chain reaction starts in Kentucky (Iroquois for "dark and bloody ground") that commences the end of the United States as we know it.

A smoldering pit twenty stories deep swallows downtown. A quarter million Americans, give or take a hundred thousand, for two miles out, die instantly, mercifully. Across the Ohio River in Indiana, Jeffersonville and New Albany are flattened. The iconic steeples of Churchill Downs, three miles south of the Seelbach, cascade in burning wreckage. The live burning horses sound no more like horses than live burning humans sound like humans.

A west wind sends the fire sheet across Crescent Hill and past St. Matthews. That evening, radiation fallout will prove four times as fatal as it needs to be in Cincinnati, up river a hundred miles, due to lack of warning.

The terrorist plot dooms Houston and Chicago as well. Total destruction encompasses both Rice University and the University of Houston, and reaches Old Spanish Trail to the south. The radiation plume heads for flood-ruined New Orleans, a hundred miles east.

Just outside one of the University of Chicago's gothic quadrangles survives Henry Moore's memorial to the first self-sustaining nuclear chain reaction, a bronze dome supported by three irregular, cliff-like legs. Here, less than seventy years ago, on December 2, 1942, jubilant scientists toasted one another on a squash court. Now the United States, the greatest military might ever known, will visit ruin in return on suspected terrorist host nations, ushering in a new dark age. Collateral to the human carnage, symbolic of the interdependence of culture and hope, the Chicago Art Institute's treasures—old masters, Renaissance, Impressionist—have incinerated, but today few care about a loss that will be regretted long after the name of every corpse is forgotten.

The reader is asked to imagine that the United States and other nations are unquestionably headed toward just such a fate. In other words, imagine for discussion's sake that, absent some drastic intervention, the worst is sure to happen. Imagine as well, however, that apocalypse could be averted if the correct policies are adopted.

The reader now is asked to answer the eight questions of Appendix E (page 227). If your answers tend to fall on the first choices rather than the second, these chapters have not been persuasive, and you are implored to figure out alternative ways to head off disaster. If your answers fall on the second choices, go see your mayor, city councilor, or alderman.

APPENDIX A

Letter to Mayor or Elected Governing Board of a City or Town

Dear Mayor _____:
(or Dear Board of Supervisors, Dear Chairperson [of a City Council or Board of Aldermen])

The undersigned request a time to discuss with you ways in which this city (town) might contribute to greater security for Americans. News reports about terrorist efforts to acquire nuclear weapons and the erosion of nonproliferation rules leave little doubt that urban populations are, or may soon be, at a greater risk than they have ever been.

The undersigned are not of one mind about what targeted populations could do about this situation, or whether anything can be done. We do, however, think that it is time for populations that terrorists may target to discuss, with other targeted populations around the world, how to reduce the risks.

Our tentative conclusion is that it would make sense for cities and towns in this country and around the world to elect municipal representatives to an annual security assembly. We would like to explore with you [or with our elected representatives on the city council or board of aldermen] the possibility of placing on our municipal ballot a slot to elect a representative to such a security assembly, assuming that a dozen or more other cities or towns in each of three or four countries will do the same.

We think that directly electing representatives from communities is the essential means of ensuring that the welfare of the threatened populations will receive first priority and avoiding any suspicion that in some countries national governments might seek to manipulate the dialogue in which their communities are participating.

Cross-border meetings between cities are of course nothing new. There are thousands of sister city relationships around the world as well as a great many formal and informal commercial and trade assemblies, conventions, pairings, and so on. [At this point insert reference to any international group that the city or town already belongs to.] Considering the stakes involved, especially nuclear proliferation, the risks of nuclear terrorism, and the present and potential targeting of cities for missile attack, interurban security conferences seem a most appropriate first measure.

Respectfully,

APPENDIX B

Resolution of Municipal Governing Board

This municipality, responding to the increasing dangers to its residents from nuclear and other means of mass killing that national governments have failed to control in the sixty-five years since the end of World War II, despite vast arming for defense, for deterrence, for power balance, and for preventive action; despite persistent efforts to organize nations both globally and regionally for purposes of greater security; despite many successes at the national level in the fields of human rights, wealth production, and fairness and understanding as to racial, gender, religious, and belief differences, concludes:

1. That the safety of its citizens transcends the security capacities of individual nations and coalitions of nations.

2. That the personal involvement of more individuals, on a global scale, will be required to achieve greater security.

3. That the only political level at which significantly more people can become actively, intellectually, and personally involved to the point at which they can influence policy and events is the municipal level.

4. That greater citizen involvement in security issues will strengthen the cohesion and security of the nation, which, like municipal and individual security, requires global security to protect itself.

As a first and experimental step, this municipality resolves to offer a place on the municipal ballot for candidates who file a nominating petition containing the names of twenty-five registered voters for the position of representative for a two-year term to an annual meeting of representatives of cities and towns in this and other nations, the initial agenda of which shall be to propose to the peoples of the world a system for organizing security around law, enforced by democratically accountable institutions that the city and town meetings shall be charged by the attached First-Year Agenda to explore.

The mayor [or chair of the governing board] is requested to write to her/his counterpart in twenty-five other communities, at least half of which shall be in other countries, to propose such a meeting.

APPENDIX C

Agenda, First Meeting of Municipal Security Assembly

I. Review how verification has proceeded under existing arms-control treaties. How to achieve acceptable assurance that phased, verified arms reductions can occur without compromising any nation's security.

- Training of inspectors, numbers required for varying intensities of inspections, costs, level of reliability

- Interplay between justified national secrecy of military research, armaments levels, and preparedness for self-defense, and the need to achieve inspection reliability

- Means to enforce inspection regimes with respect to (i) refusals to permit inspections, (ii) discovery of violations of arms limitations agreements and rules, and (iii) need for adjudication of disputed issues of compliance

- Penalties for arms-control violations: (a) forfeit of national security deposits pledged to secure compliance; (b) use of international or regional force

- Hypothetical scenarios for achieving progressive levels of arms-control verification, based on expanding levels of means of enforcement, kept in proportion to expanding international democracy as the means to assure democratic control

II. Review present state of targeting of cities by national governments. Adoption of inquiry addressed to nations known to possess WMD, asking:

- What cities do you target?

- What level of assurance would justify your detargeting of cities and pledging no WMD assault on the cities that now are targeted, and accepting international verification inspections?

- Of the cities that you have targeted, which are targeted to deter attack on you by the national governments of those cities, and which are targeted to deter the supplying of WMD to other nations or to nonstate actors such as terrorists?

- What would you offer as a security pledge to assure other nations of your compliance with your undertakings to detarget and not to target?

- What reciprocal steps by other nations would you require?

III. Review compliance with and confidence in existing treaty framework, including:

- Reductions of deployed and reserved force levels, i.e., numbers of weapons

- Renewals, replacements, and improvements of existing weapons

- Comprehensive Nuclear-Test-Ban Treaty

- Outer Space Treaty

IV. Consideration of levels of standing international forces that would be necessary to police global restrictions on arms creation, trade, possession, and deployment, assuming that the progressive buildup of enforcement capacity is matched by progressive national armaments reductions.

V. Proposals to achieve a level of democratic accountability that would justify empowering global law-enforcement capabilities:

- Review democracy exercised in electing delegates to the municipal assembly

- Proposals for offering cities packages of procedures for holding elections to obtain city representation at the conference. Inducements to cities: greater safety, opportunity to help mold the growth of the conference and influence its policies

- Adoption of means for conference to ensure bona fide election results through a review and approval process for monitoring elections and credentialing delegates

- Discussion of means to keep representation proportional to respective sizes of constituencies and the nations that they derive from

- Discussion of the extent, if any, to which population blocks should be composed of a single nationality, or a single ethnic group or geographic area without respect to nationality, keeping in mind that the conference's purpose is to enhance security from WMD attack, whether the product of war or terrorism

VI. Conference expansion proposals:

- Maximum workable size

- Techniques for accommodating growth: (a) spin off sub-assemblies that would choose the delegates to the global body; (b) rotate representation, with set terms of office (for instance, three years for a single city); (c) assign to each nation a limit on the number of its cities permitted to seat delegates (but this is not to suggest the national governments should choose the cities)

VII. Organization, staffing, and continuity

- Establish standing committees: electoral, military, legal, publicity, financial

- Staffing: based on committee structure

- Financing: municipal, foundation, individual donations (avoid financial dependence on nations)

APPENDIX D

President's Speech

I am calling on Americans for their individual assistance in helping to stabilize the world. If the United States is to influence the outcome of the conflicts going on in the world today, and if those conflicts are to be resolved peacefully, a great many American citizens as well as citizens of other nations must become involved.

Some of the conflicts endanger our nation and our way of life. They cannot be won by force of arms. If winning wars were the answer, in a sense it would be easier, because we know how to win wars. What we must win now, though, must be won without war, because war in the nuclear age can have no winners. For the foreseeable future we will not let down our nuclear guard because it is one of the ways in which to deter nuclear attacks on us by nations and to a limited degree by terrorists, at least to the extent that nuclear weapons can be traced. This hair-trigger approach to security, though, must in the long run be replaced by more reliable security, by safer ways to manage conflicts. With deterrable foes, error may defeat deterrence. With terrorists—foes that may not be deterred—we must slice away their support until they collapse.

If I had a blueprint for security in the world of today and tomorrow, I would not be making the request to you that I am going to make. Before getting to that, I want you to know what I am worried about as part of my concern about the doomsday nature of modern war.

I am concerned that the increased complexity of public affairs will lead to civic enfeeblement. Democracy as the founders gave it to us assumed that most citizens—in fact all citizens in possession of health and independence—would share responsibility for how their society performed. I am concerned that the complexities of technology, economics, environmental threats, and the global nature of so many policy decisions have diminished our mutual confidence that, working together as a free people, we can solve the problems and remove the threats that confront us.

I am concerned that Americans will, in electing their leaders, grow unable to discriminate between genuine intellect and genuine morality, and shallow, self-serving, opportunistic media-disguised puppets of profiteers and ideologues. I am concerned that demagogues and would-be tyrants will manipulate us. I am concerned because it is natural to belittle what one cannot control, and so much that must be controlled appears to be slipping out of democratic control due to the failure to separate what is vital from what is trivial and what is genuine from what is false.

I have asked some hundred informed and thoughtful people, from a variety of backgrounds and disciplines and of diverse political views, each to name twenty books they wish every American would read. I told them I was interested in books that would help Americans figure out how to make themselves more secure and contribute to greater security for other peoples. I said that I was interested in books that would help people figure out how to maintain a robust economy and full employment; how to prevent poverty; how to ensure affordable health care for all; how to create effective schools; how to preserve our environment; and how to achieve a stable civic life, with greater intensity of inquiry but less animosity, discord, and distrust.

I told them that I did not want to encroach on religion. I told them I did not want polemics or technical books. Books advocating a single point of view would be fine as long as the author was intellectually honest about what she or he advocated. Books addressing opposing points of view would be welcome, because asking the right questions is more valuable than pretending to have the right answers.

These hundred one-time advisors were chosen without regard for party preference. None are part of my administration and none of them work for the federal government. They include elected officials, business leaders, union leaders, teachers, scholars, scientists, and engineers. I omitted people best known for zealous advocacy of a single viewpoint, whether I happened to agree with that viewpoint or not, because I wanted objective, analytical books. However, I included people who are persuaded of the soundness of one policy or another, and these advisors certainly represent not a few opposing views on particular policies. I instructed them to make no recommendation that might benefit them personally.

Almost all of the hundred people responded, and all told, they suggested _____ books. A list of all those books is available on a new website, together with the authors and the names of the one hundred persons I consulted, though not matched with their recommended book titles. Many books were named by more than one person, and when several suggested the same book, that was persuasive, though not conclusive, for including it on the final list. When I had the names of several titles in the same general subject matter, I asked the opinions of people in the field as to which would prove most useful to the general public. The decisions leading to a final list of twenty books were mine in the end.

Here is a list of the twenty books. I am asking every American to read these books over the next two years, to read them and discuss them with neighbors, friends, family, and fellow workers.

Critics will have a field day telling you that Author A would have been a better choice than Author B, or suggesting ulterior motives for including one book rather than another. Great! The more discussion the better. I do not want to hear, though, that Americans haven't time to read, or that the books are too difficult, or that it is my job and not yours to be smart. Most

Americans have gone to high school and millions to college. There are few high school graduates who cannot handle these books.

If you want to substitute other books for some of those on the list, fine, but please make sure that any substitute covers the same topics, and if someone tells you to substitute a book, made sure that you are not being manipulated into a certain belief or "protected" from another.

I am sure that I will wind up reading some of the books that people say should have been included but were not. And by the way, no, I have not read all twenty books, but I promise to do so over the next two years, and I promise to discuss them with you, on the blog we have created for everyone's use, in my addresses and legislative proposals, and in community meetings.

APPENDIX E
(see page 214)

Eight Questions to Assess Reader's Readiness

For each pair of statements, place an *x* the box next to the one you *most* agree with.

1. [ ] It is human nature to fight, so it never will be possible entirely to prevent war.

   [ ] Most people in the world live peacefully their entire lives, so peace clearly would be attainable if governments cooperated to create enforced law.

2. [ ] The world is too large and people and cultures too diverse ever to submit to a common regime of law enforcement.

   [ ] Given that countries as large and diverse as the United States can submit to common legal rules, no reason exists, given today's technological advances, why law and order could not encompass the world.

3. [ ] Some people are inherently evil, and some of them always will find a way to foment war.

   [ ] Whether some people are born evil and beyond redemption is irrelevant, as many societies have proved that criminals can be prevented from taking over governments and running society.

4. [ ] The United States conducts its foreign relations legally, with the highest priority given to keeping peace in the world and keeping Americans secure.

   [ ] Much of American foreign policy serves corporate and interest-group interests as well as militaristic theory and

ideology, ahead of the long-term security needs of the American people.

5. [ ] The long-term security needs of Americans are best met through military alliances and waging war against any who threaten our vital interests and those of our allies.

    [ ] Even if the ability to win wars formerly served our best interests, our best interests today, despite the need to maintain an effective defense and deterrence posture, lies in preventing war and controlling WMD through law enforcement.

6. [ ] International law enforcement and war prevention, to the extent they are possible, can only be accomplished by military alliances, and it would be dangerous to endow the UN or another international body with a military force large enough to enforce peace and resolve disputes worldwide.

    [ ] Military alliances cannot keep peace dependably because they are inherently polarizing.

7. [ ] Even if accountable global peacekeeping were feasible, it would require decades to put in place, and in the meantime the United States, as the strongest nation, must continue to play the role of leading enforcer.

    [ ] Our enforcement efforts are backfiring because they polarize the power centers of the world, so the best policy in the short run as well as the long run would be to start the decades-long process of erecting a global system of enforced law, and to show our own willingness to submit to enforced law by submitting to the first steps of verified arms control and peace enforcement.

8. [ ] The United States political system cannot significantly be improved on, and in any event, if I vote in elections at all three levels of government, I have done all that one person can do.

    [ ] I do not believe that voting is enough, given the dangers we face, and the effect that voting was meant to have is often thwarted due to money, media influence, and gerrymandering.

Bibliography

2020 Vision Campaign. 2008. www.2020visioncampaign.org

Ackerman, Bruce, and James S. Fishkin. 2004. *Deliberation Day* (New Haven, CT: Yale University Press).

Adams, James. 1990. *Engines of War: Merchants of Death and the New Arms Race* (New York: Atlantic Monthly Press).

Alger, Chadwick F. 1993. "Protecting Local Autonomy in a Global Constitutional Order," in *The Constitutional Foundations of World Peace*, ed. Richard A. Falk, Robert C. Johansen, and Samuel S. Kim (Albany: State University of New York).

Alperovitz, Gar. 1995. *The Decision to Use the Atomic Bomb and the Architecture of an American Myth* (New York: Knopf).

———. 2007. "California Split," in *New York Times*, February 10.

Alvarez, José E. 2005. *International Organizations as Law-Makers* (New York: Oxford University Press).

Anderson, Clinton P. 1970. *Outsider in the Senate: Senator Clinton Anderson's Memoirs* (New York: World).

Archibugi, Daniele. 1995. "From the United Nations to Cosmopolitan Democracy," in *Cosmopolitan Democracy: An Agenda for a New World Order*, ed. Daniele Archibugi and David Held (Cambridge, Eng.: Polity Press).

Bache, Ian, and Matthew Flinders. 2004. "Multi-level Governance: Conclusions and Implications," in *Multi-Level Governance* (Oxford, Eng.: Oxford University Press).

Barash, David R. 2003. "The Disparity Between Biological and Cultural Evolution in the Pursuit of Peace," in *The Future of Peace in the Twenty-First Century*, ed. Nicholas N. Kittrie, Rodrigo Carazo, and James R. Mancham (Durham, NC: Carolina Academic Press).

Barash, David R., and Judith Eve Lipton. 1982. *Stop Nuclear War! A Handbook* (New York: Grove Press).

Baratta, Joseph Preston. 2004. *The Politics of World Federation* (Westport, CT, and London: Praeger).

Barber, Benjamin. 1984. *Strong Democracy: Participatory Politics for a New Age* (Berkeley: University of Califiornia Press).

———. 1995. *Jihad vs. McWorld* (New York: Ballantine).

———. 1998. *A Passion for Democracy: American Essays* (Princeton, NJ: Princeton University Press).

Bell, David. 2007. *The First Total War: Napoleon's Europe and the Birth of Modern Warfare* (Boston: Houghton Mifflin).

Bellamy, Richard, and R. J. Barry Jones. 2000. "Globalization and Democracy: An Afterword," in *Global Democracy: Key Debates*, ed. Barry Holden (New York: Routledge).

Benjamin, Daniel, and Steven Simon. 2005. *The Next Attack: The Failure of the War on Terror and a Strategy for Getting It Right* (New York: Owl Books/Henry Holt).

Bobbitt, Philip. 2008. *Terror and Consent: The Wars for the Twenty-First Century* (New York: Knopf).

Boulding, Elise. 1993. "IGOs, the UN, and International NGOs: The Evolving Ecology of the International System," in *The Constitutional Foundations of World Peace*, ed. Richard A. Falk, Robert C. Johansen, and Samuel S. Kim (Albany: State University of New York).

Bozorgmehir, Najmeh. 2008. "Teheran Mayor's Ambition Lies within City Limits," in *Financial Times*, January 9.

Bradley, Bill. 2007. *The New American Story* (New York: Random House).

Broder, John M. 2007. "Governors Join in Creating Regional Pacts on Climate Change," in *New York Times*, November 15.

Brzezinski, Zbigniew. 1997. *The Grand Chessboard: American Primacy and Its Geostrategic Imperatives* (New York: Basic Books).

———. 2007. *Second Chance: Three Presidents and the Crisis of American Superpower* (New York: Basic Books).

Burns, Robert. 2007. "Civilian Role Urged in War on Terrorism," in *Boston Globe*, November 27.

Cabasso, Jackie. 2008. "US Conference of Mayors Adopts Resolution for the Elimination of Nuclear Weapons by 2020," 2020 Vision Campaign, June 28. www.2020visioncampaign.org

Carlton, Jim. 2008. "Nine Cities, Nine Ideas," in *Wall Street Journal*, February 11.

Caro, Robert A. 1982. *The Years of Lyndon Johnson: The Path to Power* (New York: Knopf).

Carr, Edward Hallett. 1962. *What Is History?* (New York: Knopf).

Childers, Erskine, and Brian Urquhart. 1994. *Renewing the United Nations System* (Uppsala, Sweden: Dag Hammarskjöld Foundation).

Clark, Grenville, and Louis B. Sohn. 1966. *World Peace Through World Law*, 3rd ed. (Cambridge, MA: Harvard University Press).

Commission on Global Governance. 1995. *Our Global Neighborhood: Report of the Commission on Global Governance* (Oxford, Eng.: Oxford University Press).

Council of Europe. 2000. *Participation of Citizens in Local Public Life* (Strasbourg, France: Council of Europe Publishing).

———. 2006. *European Charter of Local Self-Government: 20th Anniversary.* Congress of Local and Regional Authorities, Local and Regional Action No. 8. (Strasbourg, France: Council of Europe Publishing).

Crawford, Leslie. 2007. *Financial Times,* May 26–27.

Dahl, Robert A., and E. R. Tufte. 1973. *Size and Democracy* (Stanford, CA: Stanford University Press).

Delmas, Philippe. 1997. *The Rosy Future of War* (New York: Free Press).

Dionne, E. J. Jr. 1991. *Why Americans Hate Politics* (New York: Touchstone/Simon & Schuster).

Eilperin, Juliet. 2006. "Cities, States Take Lead on Global Warming," in *Boston Globe,* August 13.

Eisenhower, Dwight D. 1956. *Public Papers of the President of the United States: Dwight D. Eisenhower, 1956* (Washington, DC: U.S. Government Printing Office).

Erskine, John. 1916. *The Moral Obligation to Be Intelligent* (New York: Duffield).

Falk, Richard. 1975. *A Global Approach to National Policy* (Cambridge, MA: Harvard University Press).

———. 1986. *Nuclear Weapons and the Future of Humanity: The Fundamental Questions* (Totowa, NJ: Rowman and Allanheld).

———. 1995. *On Humane Governance: Toward a New Global Politics* (University Park: Pennsylvania State University Press).

———. 2000. "Global Civil Society and the Democratic Prospect," in *Global Democracy: Key Debates,* ed. Barry Holden (New York: Routledge).

Falk, Richard, and David Krieger, ed.. 2008. *At the Nuclear Precipice: Catastrophe or Transformation?* (London: Palgrave Macmillan).

Federalist, The. 1961. Ed. Jacob E. Cooke. (Middletown, CT: Wesleyan University Press).

Feinstein, Lee, and Ann Marie Slaughter. 2004. "A Duty to Prevent," in *Foreign Affairs* 83 (January/February).

Fishkin, James S. n.d. "Deliberative Polling®: Toward a Better-Informed Democracy." http://cdd.stanford.edu/polls/docs/summary.

Friedrich, Carl Joachim. 1948. *Inevitable Peace* (Cambridge, MA: Harvard University Press).

Fukuyama, Francis. 2006. *America at the Crossroads: Democracy, Power, and the Neoconservative Legacy* (New Haven, CT: Yale University Press).

Fung, Archon. 2004. *Empowered Participation: Reinventing Urban Democracy* (Princeton, NJ: Princeton University Press).

Gardner, John W. 1961. *Excellence: Can We Be Equal and Excellent Too?* (New York: Harper & Row).

Garrahan, Matthew. 2008. "Mayor Sets Agenda for Nation," in *Financial Times*, October 28.

Goodby, James E. 2007. Quoted in *Brookings Institution Bulletin*, February 4.

Gorbachev, Mikhail. 2000. *On My Country and the World* (New York: Columbia University Press).

Hanley, Charles J. 2007. "Hybrid Taxis," in *Boston Globe*, December 8.

Harris, Sam. 2004. *The End of Faith: Religion, Terror, and the Future of Reason* (London: Norton).

Held, David. 1995. *Democracy and the Global Order: From the Modern State to Cosmopolitan Governance* (Stanford, CA: Stanford University Press).

Herbert, Bob. 2007. "Hooked on Violence," in *Boston Globe*, April 26.

Hersey, John. 1946. *Hiroshima* (New York: Knopf).

Huntington, Samuel P. 1996. *The Clash of Civilizations and the Remaking of World Order* (New York: Simon & Schuster).

Janis, Mark W. 2003. *An Introduction to International Law*. 4th ed. (New York: Aspen).

Johnson, Chalmers. 2006. *Nemesis: The Last Days of the American Republic* (New York: Henry Holt).

Jungk, Robert. 1961. *Children of the Ashes: The Story of Rebirth*, trans. Constintine Fitzgibbons (New York: Harcourt Brace & World).

Kaldor, Mary. 1995. "European Institutions, Nation-States, and Nationalism," in *Cosmopolitan Democracy: An Agenda for a New World Order*, ed. Daniele Archibugi and David Held (Cambridge, Eng.: Polity Press).

Kant, Immanuel. 1948. "Eternal Peace," in Carl Joachim Friedrich, *Inevitable Peace* (Cambridge, MA: Harvard University Press).

Kaplan, Robert D. 2001. *The Coming Anarchy: Shattering the Dreams of the Post Cold War* (New York: Vintage).

Kedourie, Elie. 1993. *Nationalism*, 4th ed. (Oxford, Eng.: Blackwell).

Kiesling, John Brady. 2006. *Diplomacy Lessons: Realism for an Unloved Superpower* (Washington, DC: Potomac Books).

Klosterman, Chuck. 2007. "America," in *Esquire*, January.

Köchler, Hans. 2000. In *Concepts of Democratic Citizenship* (Council of Europe Publishing).

Kohn, Hans. 1955. *Nationalism* (Princeton, NJ: D. Van Nostrand).

Kronholz, June. 2006. "The Coming Crunch," in *Wall Street Journal*, October 13.

Kropotkin, Peter A. 1970. "The State: Its Historic Role," in *Selected Writings on Anarchism and Revolution*, ed. Martin A. Miller (Cambridge, MA: MIT Press).

Langewiesche, William. 2007. *The Atomic Bazaar: The Rise of the Nuclear Poor* (New York: Farrar Straus Giroux).

Lapham, Lewis H. 1990. *Imperial Masquerade* (New York: Grove Weidenfeld).

Lapp, R. E. 1949. *Must We Hide?* (Cambridge, MA: Addison-Wesley).

Machiavelli, Niccolo. 1940. *The Prince and the Discourses* (New York: Modern Library).

Marks, Gary, and Liesbet Hooghe. 2004. "Contrasting Visions of Multi-Level Governance," in *Multi-Level Governance*, ed. Ian Bache and Matthew Flinders (Oxford, Eng.: Oxford University Press).

Mead, Margaret. 2003. "Warfare as an Invention," in *The Future of Peace in the Twenty-First Century*, ed. Nicholas N. Kittrie, Rodrigo Carazo, and James R. Mancham (Durham, NC: Carolina Academic Press).

Miller, Perry, ed. 1962. *The Legal Mind in America: From Independence to the Civil War* (Garden City, NY: Doubleday)

Mills, C. Wright. 1956. *The Power Elite* (New York: Oxford University Press).

———. 1960. *The Causes of World War Three* (New York: Ballantine).

Morgan, Edmund S. 1988. *Inventing the People: The Rise of Popular Sovereignty in England and America* (New York: Norton).

Mumford, Lewis. 1961. *The City in History: Its Origins, Its Transformations, and Its Prospects* (New York: Harcourt, Brace & World).

Nerfin, Marc. 1993. "United Nations: Prince and Citizen?" in *The Constitutional Foundations of World Peace*, ed. Richard A. Falk, Robert C. Johansen, and Samuel S. Kim (Albany: State University of New York).

Newman, William J. 1964. *Liberalism and the Retreat from Politics* (New York: Braziller).

NLC [National League of Cities]. 2003. http://www.nlc.org/home/.

Núñez, Joseph R. 2007. "One NATO Is Not Enough," in *New York Times*, January 27.

NWC [Nuclear Weapons Convention]. 2008. http://www .2020visionscampaign.org/pages/.

Page, Benjamin I., and Marshall M. Boulton. 2006. *The Foreign Policy Dis-Connect: What Americans Want from Our Leaders But Don't Get* (Chicago: University of Chicago Press).

Palmer, Frederick. 1934. *Bliss, Peacemaker: The Life and Letters of General Tasker Howard Bliss* (New York: Dodd, Mead).

Patterson, Walter. 1984. *The Plutonium Business and the Spread of the Bomb* (San Francisco: Sierra Club).

Perkins, John A. 1981. *The Prudent Peace: Law as Foreign Policy* (Chicago: University of Chicago Press).

Peters, B. Guy, and Jon Pierre. 2004. "Multi-Level Governance and Democracy: A Faustian Bargain?" in *Multi-Level Governance*, ed. Ian Bache and Matthew Flinders (Oxford, Eng.: Oxford University Press).

Pfaff, William. 1994. *The Wrath of Nations* (New York: Touchstone/ Simon & Schuster)

———. *Boston Globe*, September 15, 2003

Purcell Jr., Edward A. 2007. *Originalism, Federalism, and the American Constitutional Enterprise: A Historical Inquiry* (New Haven, CT: Yale University Press).

Putnam, Robert D. 1993. *Making Democracy Work: Civic Traditions in Modern Italy* (Princeton, NJ: Princeton University Press).

Riesman, David, Nathan Glazer, and Reuel Denney. 1950. *The Lonely Crowd: A Study of the Changing American Character* (Hartford, CT: Yale University Press).

Rochlin, Gene I. 1979. *Plutonium, Power, and Politics: International Arrangements for the Disposition of Spent Nuclear Fuel* (Berkeley: University of California Press).

Rhodes, Richard. 2007. *Arsenals of Folly: The Making of the Nuclear Arms Race* (New York, Knopf).

Rosenau, James N. 2004. "Strong Demand, Huge Supply: Governance in an Emerging Epoch," in *Multi-Level Governance*, ed. Ian Bache and Matthew Flinders (Oxford, Eng.: Oxford University Press).

Sable, Jonathan. 2008. "Tokyo Mayor Leads on Climate," in *Financial Times*, June 3.

Said, Edward. 2002. *Reflections on Exile and Other Essays* (Cambridge, MA: Harvard University Press).

Sands, Philippe. 2005. *Lawless World: America and the Making and Breaking of Global Rules from FDR's Atlantic Charter to George W. Bush's Illegal War* (New York: Viking Penguin).

Saulny, Susan. 2007. "Green Alley Program," in *New York Times*, November 26.

Schlesinger, Arthur M., Jr. 1965. *A Thousand Days: John F. Kennedy in the White House* (Boston: Houghton Mifflin).

Schneidmiller, Chris. 2008. "U.N. Chief Presses Nuclear Disarmament," in *Global Security Newswire* (Nuclear Threat Initiative), October 27. www.nti.org.

Sennett, Richard. 1977. *The Fall of Public Man* (New York: Knopf).

Shenkman, Rick. 2008. "The Dumbing Down of Voters," in *Boston Globe*, June 15.

Slack, Donovan. 2006. In *Boston Globe*, October 26.

Slevin, Peter. 2006. In *Boston Globe*, August 13.

Stern, Jessica. 2003. *Terror in the Name of God: Why Religious Militants Kill* (New York: Ecco).

Stevenson, Adlai E. 1979. *The Papers of Adlai E. Stevenson, vol. 8: Ambassador to the United Nations, 1961–1965*, ed. Walter Johnson (Boston: Little, Brown).

Stiglitz, Joseph E. 2006. *Making Globalization Work* (New York: Norton).

Stout, Jeffrey. 2004. *Democracy and Tradition* (Princeton, NJ: Princeton University Press).

Taheri, Amir. 2006. "The Perils of Engagement," in *Wall Street Journal*, May 9.

Tejera, Victorino. 1993. *The City-State Foundations of Western Political Thought* (Lanham, MD: University Press of America).

Tenet, George. 2007. *At the Center of the Storm: My Years at the CIA* (New York: HarperCollins).

Thucydides. 1996. *Peloponnesian War* (Landmark Edition), ed. Robert B. Strassler; trans. Richard Crawley (New York: Free Press/ Simon & Schuster).

Tolstoy, Leo. 1954. *War and Peace*, trans. Louise and Aylmer Maude (New York: Simon and Schuster).

UN-HABITAT. 2006. *State of the World's Cities 2006/7: The Millennium Development Goals and Urban Sustainability: 30 Years of Shaping the Habitat Agenda* (London: Earthscan).

Walker, R. B. J. 1993. "World Order and the Reconstitution of Political Life," in *The Constitutional Foundations of World Peace*, ed. Richard A. Falk, Robert C. Johansen, and Samuel S. Kim (Albany: State University of New York).

Weapons of Mass Destruction Commission. 2006. *Weapons of Terror: Freeing the World of Nuclear, Biological, and Chemical Arms* (Stockholm: Weapons of Mass Destruction Commission).

Wedel, Janine R. 2006. "Harvard's Role in US Aid to Russia," in *Boston Globe*, March 25.

Wehle, Greg. 2008. Untitled article in Global Security Newswire, September 29.

Weinstock, Daniel M. 2001. "Prospects for Transnational Citizenship and Democracy," in *Ethics & International Affairs* 15.

Welch, Stephen, and Caroline Kennedy-Pipe. 2004. "Multi-Level Governance and International Relations," in *Multi-Level Governance*, ed. Ian Bache and Matthew Flinders (Oxford, Eng.: Oxford University Press).

Wells, Charlotte C. 1995. *Law and Citizenship in Early Modern France* (Baltimore, MD: Johns Hopkins University Press).

Williams, Paul L. 2005. *The Al Qaeda Connection: International Terrorism, Organized Crime, and the Coming Apocalypse* (Amherst, NY: Prometheus Books).

York, Herbert. 1970. *Race to Oblivion: A Participant's View of the Arms Race* (New York: Simon and Schuster).

Zimmerman, Peter D., and Jeffrey G. Lewis. 2006. "The Bomb in the Backyard," *Foreign Policy*, November/December.

Index

Benjamin Franklin Trueblood,
Secretary of the American Peace
Society, 1892–1915.